Out of the Hood

Out of the Hood

THE LIFE OF THE FALCONER

MARCUS DERBYSHIRE

Coch-y-Bonddu Books
2017

OUT OF THE HOOD
The Life of the Falconer
Marcus Derbyshire

First published by Coch-y-Bonddu Books Ltd, Machynlleth, 2017

ISBN 978 1 904784 82 1

Coch-y-Bonddu Books Ltd, Machynlleth, Powys, SY20 8DG
01654 702837
www.anglebooks.com

Printed and bound in Great Britain by
TJ International Ltd, Padstow, Cornwall

Contents

I dedicate this book to my lovely daughter Emily who once remarked that she was never coming out on Bodmin Moor ever again – but continues to do so, and not even under duress.

Also to John Barr (1840-1880)

One of three brothers from a famous family of Scottish falconers, John Barr was highly skilled in all aspects of the sport. As a professional falconer his livelihood led him to be much travelled, whether providing sport in Europe, Egypt, India, or trapping gyrfalcons in Norway. Indeed he boasted a most impressive CV, not only working for some of the great names of the sport, but also as head falconer to the Champagne Hawking Club in France and also the newly formed Old Hawking Club in England.

Other aspects of his life give me a certain empathy towards him. I would like to think that if we had lived in the same age (his rather than mine), we would have been firm friends.

Acknowledgements

FIRSTLY, SPECIAL THANKS must go to John Loft and Nick Wilkinson. Without their help and assistance this book would have remained a mere pipe dream, scribbled notes in the bottom of a drawer.

- Additionally, my good friend and game hawker, Nigel Deacon, for his sterling work with the editing whilst recuperating from his near-fatal hand-gliding accident.

- Richard Waddington for his contributions and for providing great company out on the hill. A great falconer and a top man.

- Chris Galeski and Will Emerick for their splendid photographs.

- Ken McKinley for contributing his illustrations and his poem: hood-maker and all-round talented man. kenmac@gmx.com

- Heather Hope for helping out a man who is computer-illiterate and stuck in the dark ages. Thanks for all the time she spent with me in front of the screen when she would have much preferred to be at the bar – as would I!

- Friends who have taken the time to read my material with a critical eye; Nick and John, and also Paul MacKinder, Trevor Pick, and Dave Taylor. And my publisher, Paul Morgan, and his designer, Pete Mackenzie, who finally knocked it into shape.

- To my parents, family and friends who have had to put up with me and my hawks for all these years – and for all the sacrifices they have had to make at various times.

- Lisa Marriott for helping type out many extra pieces, even though she had about as much enthusiasm in front of the screen as I did.

- Lee O'Dwyer for his terrific photographs of my jack merlin, *Beeswing*, on the cover of this book.

- And finally, everyone else who has taken to the field with me, either as fellow falconers, assistants, or observers.

"He lures, he leapes, he calles, he cries, he joyes, he waxeth sad, and frames his mood according as his hawk doth well or bad."

George Turberville, 1575

It's as true today as it was then.

Preface

HOW COULD ONE possibly justify adding to the plethora of falconry books written over the past 500 years, particularly those written more recently, and certainly not the addition of another 'How to do it' manual? The books dedicated to the flying of a particular species, or covering a specific branch of the sport, have all been written several times over, although there is only one book dedicated solely to lark hawking, John Loft's excellent *A Merlin for Me*. Add to this my feelings of inadequacy, knowing full well that there are, and have been, many falconers better than me and better qualified to put pen to paper.

Despite this I have always had in the back of my mind the thought that I would one day record my thoughts and experiences on the subject, awareness of the sacrifices I have made, my anti-establishment attitude towards my elders and betters, and – having too much time on my hands – I shall take the plunge ... Here we go!

We have not used my original title for this book. The very first words I sat down and wrote were "Crown green bowling for me." The reason for the aforementioned title was that it had become a standing joke amongst a small circle of friends – when proceedings in the field were not going swimmingly the falconer in question, usually me to be fair, would utter the statement, "bloody hawks, I've had enough, I'm taking up crown green bowling!" Alas, in the end, I had to bow to peer-pressure; nobody liked the title other than me. This is not going to be a beginner's manual or a fine analysis of one particular style of flight but merely the ramblings of your average falconer taken from a life-time in the field, unusual anecdotes and occurrences, triumphs and disasters, favourite hawks and memorable flights.

I suppose, to answer my original question, it is really to try to justify it all to myself, all the sacrifices I have made, the time and effort I have put in – and no little expense. I often wonder if it was, if it is, all worth it. Should I have done something more constructive ..?

11

Foreword

Major General Jeremy Rowan, OBE, QHS (now retired)

I FIRST MET Marcus Derbyshire when a mutual friend asked me if I would be interested in seeing trained hawks fly. I was intrigued, and jumped at the chance. My sole previous experience had been a staged display (nothing to do with real falconry, so Marcus told me), at the National Armouries in Leeds.

We arranged to meet just outside York and I was treated to something special. I refer not only to the stunning hawks with their (this from a military bloke) almost magical target acquisition system, the sheer elegance of the flight, but also to the wonderful and unique bond between hawk and falconer.

We flew several hawks that day and on subsequent occasions.

I have taken the opportunity to try to understand the art of the falconer over a very few small beers with Marcus. Despite being a lifelong Manchester City fan, Marcus lives and breathes falconry. He started as a boy with a hobby, the boy became dedicated to the mystery of his field.

He has read voraciously anything relevant, and has combined written wisdom with his own experience. I think this book (the subtitle of which could be *The life of a very modern falconer*) encapsulates not only the knowledge but most importantly the passion.

These hawks are Marcus's dependents. He attends their every need, and even lives with them in his stealth camper van. I can only imagine the sense of loss when he loses one, as sadly described in several places in this book.

Although this book appears to be mainly for fellow enthusiasts, I believe it should appeal to a much wider audience, who, like myself, are painfully ignorant of the grace and beauty of this ancient sport.

This book is as deep and fascinating as its author.

CHAPTER ONE

Beginning of the End

MY PARENTS, ALONG with the rest of my family, grandparents, uncles, and aunts were all City folk – Mancunians born and bred. Though my parents have always loved the countryside and the isolated places around the British Isles, they would, I think, be the first to admit that their interest in and knowledge of natural history, the fauna and flora of the land, is negligible. When I was a young lad the family relocated to the rural Midlands, close to the Warwickshire-Worcestershire border. We temporarily lived in the Lodge at the entrance to the drive of Wasthills House, one of the two country mansions on Wasthills Lane.

The Lodge provided me with two of my earliest memories.

Someone had kindly, if misguidedly, given my father a hare for the pot. (I have no knowledge of the method used to procure it). He placed it in a large walk-in pantry/cool-room, laid out on a concrete surface. I can recall being absolutely fascinated by it, staring at it for what seemed like hours, touching its fur, its ears. I think it remained there for a day or two and then it was gone. I never did know what became of it, but I know for a fact that we did not eat it. Knowing my dad I expect he gave it a decent burial somewhere in the grounds.

My second vivid recollection of this time was of seeing the Hunt, in all its splendour, coming down the lane. I couldn't take my eyes off the scene, quite alien to anything I'd ever seen before – the grandeur of it all – the horses looked enormous, their riders resplendent in their red jackets, and I had never seen so many dogs. I remained glued to the round window at the back of the Lodge until the whole entourage had gone out of sight.

These early memories, combined with the surroundings, the deciduous woodland, arable and pasture land, ponds and canals, all fuelled my interest in its wild inhabitants, the amazing proliferation of bird life. But what were they all? I still remember my first book, purchased out of my not-so-hard-earned pocket-money, the RSPB *Guide to British Birds*. It was followed by its sister publication, the RSPB *Guide to British Birds, their Nests and Eggs*. It was still an age where most boys growing up in the countryside collected birds' eggs. When we were back at school we would talk about the nests we had found the previous evening or week-end and swap eggs with each other. Fortunately most normal boys, myself included, would grow out of egg-collecting sooner or later. (Jourdain Society take note!)

I joined the YOC (Young Ornithologists' Club) and in time learned to identify the various species, to know where they could be found, and which birds inhabited the region where we lived. One of the delights of our annual holidays to Cornwall was seeing species that could not be found in the Midlands. As well as the seabirds and waders, there were buzzards (then an extreme rarity in England north of Devon), rock pipits, and stonechats – still one of my favourite birds. Like buzzards, peregrines were much scarcer back then. I can't remember when I saw my first one in the wild. I don't know why, but even then I was fascinated by birds of prey; they were my favourite birds. A mystery surrounded them, perhaps because, with the exception of the ubiquitous kestrel, they were so rarely seen.

My parents had one of those big green encyclopaedias on the bookshelf which I was idly thumbing through one evening when I came across a section entitled *Hawking* – not lengthy, not even half a page – but I read it through with astonishment. Hawks can be trained to catch wild quarry! Wow! Was this just something from olden times or did such a sport still exist today? Was it still possible to obtain a hawk? And where from? Was it legal? Where and how could I find out about it?

The following Saturday it was a bus-ride to town to scour the book-shops to see if I could find out any more information on the subject. No

Google back then! I actually found a copy of Woodford's *Manual of Falconry* which, if memory serves me, cost me £8. Then, straight back home. I couldn't put it down – I read it avidly from cover to cover and then back again. Taking it all in, and learning all these new words, was almost like learning another language. I studied the photographs in awe, my favourite one being of the magnificent female goshawk on a ring-perch on a superior lawn with a wire-haired pointer lying next to her. More books followed: Michell, Mavrogordato, Salvin and Broderick, Salvin and Freeman, Thames Valley Press reprints of other old works, and so on. A year or more passed – and many more books – before my parents finally relented and allowed me to buy a hawk (my iconoclastic nature was such that, one way or another, I would have bought one anyway). This was not without sacrifice for my parents. The garage had to double as a temporary mews, meaning my dad had to leave his car out on the drive. The garage adjoined the kitchen; in my naivety I thought that any noise would disturb the hawk. I remember my mum making tea for the family on that first evening, desperately trying not to make a sound!

I was a county player and had just broken into open-age semi-professional football, with ongoing interest from several professional clubs. I was an above-average scrum-half and a keen all-round sportsman. But, to my father's chagrin, all that went out of the window. I wanted to fly hawks – and so I did. That decision shaped the rest of my life.

CHAPTER TWO

The Hawking Year – Lark to Gull

LE HAUT VOL has always been regarded as the pinnacle of falconry, but the grand flights at cranes, herons and kites have been consigned to the pages of history, certainly in the British Isles. Having said that, I wonder if, with the current explosion in kite numbers, the sport could return? What a thrill it would be to see a hawk, or a cast of hawks, taking on *Milvus milvus*! Would Natural England issue me with a licence? How many kites would I be allowed to take? Would someone lend me an owl? Okay, I guess I'm drifting off into the realms of fantasy again.

Rooks and crows still provide the classic flight, but only a handful of individuals are fortunate enough to be able to hawk them in the few remaining areas where true ringing flights are still possible. That leaves the present-day falconer with the humble gull and the revered skylark. Despite the changes in quarry during the centuries, the principles of the flight and the aspirations of the falconer remain the same. When the high ringing flight is obtained it makes a breathtaking spectacle, with quarry and hawk striving for aerial supremacy. The two contestants ascend, usually flying in different styles and often in different directions, so markedly that the uninitiated may question whether the hawk is in fact actually flying the quarry. Once the hawk has reached parity there are cuts and slashes, short stoops and throwups and sometimes long vertical stoops – certainly in lark-hawking when the beaten lark often bails for cover on the ground.

My gull-hawking season usually ends in early to mid-March. At this time of year gulls become increasingly hard to find over the land, mostly arable, that I have flown over throughout the winter. Adult gulls are dispersing to breed and crops are beginning to grow. Gulls dislike loafing on such ground, preferring short-cropped grass, plough, or tarmac areas such as airfields and industrial estates. This change in their numbers and habits coincides with the onset of the moult and so I, for one, am happy to conclude my season. At the end of the gull-hawking season the abiding feeling is, for me, one of relief. To have reached the end of the season without any major disaster, to have enjoyed some good sport and to put the hawks down to moult fit and well and in good feather brings contentment. Any falconer achieving this in the modern day can give himself a metaphorical pat on the back.

Spring and early summer can be a period for relaxing, checking out the surf, rather than the flying conditions occupying my first thoughts of the day. But it is also time to make an inventory check on all hawking furniture – service telemetry equipment, re-varnish blocks, purchase new bells and hoods if necessary, and make up new jesses and aylmeri. On the subject of jesses it will not go amiss of me to mention my leather of choice. A few years ago I began to use yak leather and since then have used nothing else. In my opinion the necessary qualities of strength and suppleness in yak are second to none. It is available from *The Identity Store*. It goes without saying that all equipment should be kept scrupulously clean throughout the season.

There is a small bunch of enthusiasts in Britain today who annually dedicate a couple of months of their lives to lark-hawking and therefore to keeping this traditional branch of the sport from dying out altogether. Several of this merry band, myself included, would not be participating at all were it not for Nick Wilkinson, the country's most dedicated and successful breeder of merlins. The time and effort Nick puts in, year after year, to producing top quality merlins, is unmatched. He does not expend it for financial gain but for the pleasure he derives from successes in his drive towards perfection and from supplying a number of merlin-men with their hawks. An additional reward is the constant flow of e-mails during the short season about the progress of different hawks, and the levels of sport attained, culminating in the chance for him to see it for himself at the annual field-meeting at Ribblehead.

Despite already stating that I enjoy the relaxation of the close season, as April progresses we all find ourselves involved in the news from Nick about the breeding behaviour of his pairs of merlins, and our thoughts begin to wander towards those glorious late summer evenings on the moor to be followed by a cold beer (or two) as we discuss the day's sport.

Unless any other hawks are to be added to my mews, the beginning of my hawking year is defined by a particular day, usually on the week-end of the third week in July when a number of lucky merlin-men congregate up at Nick's for the annual barbecue and, more importantly, (sorry Rosey), to collect our merlins. Rich, coming across from Accrington, always seems to be the first to arrive. I'm beginning to think he camps out in Nick's front garden overnight, just so as he can have first choice of the young hawks. Despite living in the closest proximity to Nick, I am invariably either the last to arrive, or I arrive on the wrong day altogether. Struggling to drive past the Moor and Pheasant without popping in may have something to do with that! When I've never been very good at choosing a hawk from an aviary full of them, being last in the queue does not matter, for there's very little to choose between these youngsters; they all look perfect, as good aviary-bred merlins as you are ever likely to see.

Despite having half the Summer to get ourselves organised, it's amazing that every year there is always someone short of something; either leather, eyelets, back-pack, or a hood. I must confess that in years gone by I have been as guilty as anyone. But, between us, we manage to furnish all our new charges, pose for the obligatory team photograph, and wish each other good luck and good hawking before dispersing to our various regions of the country. Basing myself in Cornwall for the lark-hawking season these days, on my way there I drop off a couple of merlins to Dave and Rodney, the Devon lads.

Incidentally, I don't suppose that these musings will filter through to the powers-that-be but, in case they do, can we have August included on our lark licences please? Give us August in exchange for the last four and a half to five months and we will all be happy men. (Well, maybe apart from the merlin-man second to none in our day – and taker of winter larks. Take a bow, Mr Haggar!)

The lark-hawking season coincides with the training of any non-merlin additions to the mews, and the latter stages of the season also overlap with bringing the intermewed hawks back into condition. The moulted hawks must be enseamed. To do this, a course of food of lower nutritional value, rangle, and two or three weeks of work to the kite and the lure are enough to rid them of their summer excess and have the hawks ready for their first flights at gulls by early October.

"If hawks are short of work and not in good wind, they cannot compete successfully with such a quarry as the seagull, with its untiring buoyant flight."   W H St Quintin (c. 1890).*

The Reverend William Willimott, Rector of St Michael Caerhays Church in Cornwall was a 19th century gull-hawker. He took eyasses locally from Dodman and Parc Camels in the parish of Veryan, preferring the hawks from the former. As well as his hawks he had quite a menagerie, including an otter and two badgers. In 1876 he was given a passage hawk called *Acrobat* by Major Hawkins Fisher that had not taken to rook-hawking, and Willimott entered her to gulls. He recorded this in his *Cornish Sketchbook*:

"One notable flight was at a strong herring gull starting from Bessy Benath Tollgate in the parish of Veryan. Acrobat having missed her first stoop, the gull took the air and rang up, trying at the same time to get seawards – I ran my best – and just over Nicholls mill was clutched at a great height and was not quite dead when I reached them. This was the best flight I ever witnessed with a trained hawk."

*(More detailed information on St Quintin can be found in Roger Upton's excellent book, *A Bird in the Hand*).

It was a dozen years or more ago that my thoughts turned to gulls as an alternative to corvids. I had grown increasingly frustrated in attempting to obtain quality flights at corvids in, admittedly, less than perfect country. High stylish flights seemed to be few and far between, with most flights descending into rat-hunts or culminating into taking out the receiver and tracking the hawk down on her quarry. Finishes like this were all the more frustrating when I had spent an hour or more driving round looking for the perfect slip, deliberating over the pros and cons of each one. I trawled through my collection of books, old and new, but in the majority of them gull-hawking got barely a mention, if mentioned at all. E B Michell makes a few remarks on gull-hawking and I have to say that I now disagree with some of them (the likes of me questioning the late, great Edward Blair Michell – he must be positively rotating in his grave!). After his own comments, most of what he writes is about the work done by Mr W H St Quintin. Blaine has a few pages on the subject and makes some very valid points, although most of them are on passage hawks flown in a cast. Mavrogordato does likewise and I have to agree with both of them where the flight at the black-headed gull is concerned.

A frequently made comment was that gulls could not be flown in strong winds as they are virtually uncatchable, and the hawks are liable to be lost downwind. (Obviously in pre-telemetry days).

But it was reading about William Herbert St Quintin's exploits that really fired my enthusiasm, all the more so because he lived in Yorkshire and flew his hawks at gulls over the Yorkshire Wolds. Living in the same region myself, aspiring to follow in the footsteps of one of the great falconers of the past and flying over the same land at the same quarry (albeit in my own small way), was, and still is, a very exciting prospect indeed. Incidentally, he lost a passage hawk, *Nerissa*, in 1895 at Winteringham (it was picked up by a keeper later that day) in the same area where I had a gull-hawk electrocuted, but more of that later.

The main advantage in flying at gulls rather than corvids is that the requirements for the flight at gulls contain considerably fewer variables. Unlike corvids, gulls rarely, if ever, use any other refuge than water. Therefore areas where there may be too much cover for a flight at corvids can still provide sporting flights at gulls. All is well as long as the gulls are not on the coast or in close proximity to huge stretches of inland water from which they cannot be driven. Then there is every chance that the flight can be kept in view. I can only recall one occasion when a gull has bailed for cover, and I think that then it only crashed into the hedge attempting to make the adjacent ditch that held a few inches of water.

So, with my mind made up, it was time to switch from corvids to gulls – but I still did not know which hawk best suited for the task. Having always been somewhat of a 'big four' specialist, I finally decided to drag myself, metaphorically kicking and screaming, into the modern world. A few falconers, Dave Taylor amongst them, had done well with peregrine x saker hybrids, and these hawks seemed to have all the attributes necessary for the flight – the speed and aggression of the peregrine combined with the added size, lower wing-loading and extra perseverance of the saker. Thus, my first gull-hawk was going to be a peregrine x saker – from good parents. As well as taking care that a hawk of mine is bought from a breeder of quality youngsters, I also like to know the history of the parents and what, if they were flown, they achieved in the field. Many people don't even consider this when buying a hawk, but if they were going to buy a working dog it would be one of the first questions asked. I wouldn't buy a hawk from a breeder I didn't know, unless he was recommended by a friend, or I had seen for myself the exploits of one or more of the progeny of his breeding stock. Nothing is set in stone, of course; it doesn't necessarily follow that a hawk bred from exceptional parents will prove to be just as good, but there must be a greater chance that it will turn out well than one bred from mediocre parents. Just look at the success of the hawks that came from Lundy in the early 20th Century.

I think many falconers in our times, after buying a hawk for the field that failed to make the grade, have retired it to an aviary for breeding. The knock-on effect of this practice is the breeding of substandard hawks down the line. Remember that the hawks belonging to competent falconers that don't make the grade in the field would probably be amongst the 75% mortality-rate if they were in the wild. Back in the 19th Century heyday of the Old Hawking Club they might have started the season with a dozen fresh hawks. One or two of them might have turned out to be star performers, the same number have shown enough promise to be retained for the next season, and the rest, if not lost, be discarded in favour of fresh hawks obtained later in the year. These were predominantly passage-hawks. By contrast the average 21st Century falconer buys one hawk. He pays his money and takes his choice! Bearing this in mind, he should take every consideration into account that can shorten the odds on his hawk becoming a good one before he parts with his hard-earned cash. As I suggested, there are no guarantees. For example, many years ago my friend Nigel bought two tiercels, brothers, reared together. He trained them both in exactly the same way and one turned out to be a decent hawk while his brother was pretty well useless and acquired the name, *Sod*. Even their temperaments were total opposites.

However, I have digressed from my subject of the choice of a peregrine x saker for my first gull-hawk. Let me reiterate that I am not laying down any hard and fast rules here, just discussing my own experiences and the hawks I have flown. I am aware that falconers have had good results with some of the other hybrids such as gyr x peregrine and gyr x saker, but, despite the merits of hybrids, I presently fly a jerkin, much preferring pure-bred hawks and this particular hawk is certainly distinguishing himself in the field.

Once the process of training the would-be gull-hawk is out of the way and a degree of fitness attained, it is time for the possibly problematic business of entering. No problem of course if you happen to have a natural 'star performer' on your hands – a hawk that from the outset just wants to kill any bird it sees and not stop flying until it has done so. All it needs is to learn the correct quarry. Such a hawk is a rare gem indeed, a little fine tuning to get the hawk wedded to the correct quarry is all that is required. I use white lures from the outset and gulls as 'dead lures' once the hawk is flying free, whether that be in the traditional sense or to the kite. I use the smaller gulls initially, as young hawks can be intimidated by the larger ones, landing a few feet away from them, rather than binding to them, and then approaching with great caution.

Although wild peregrines can and sometimes do kill gulls, mainly the smaller species (indeed Ratcliffe noted a pair on a Scottish moor feeding their eyasses exclusively on black-headed gulls), they are far from being a preferred quarry for most peregrines. There are good reasons for this – the larger species are a potentially dangerous quarry, being both well-armed and often having substantial back-up from the rest of the flock. A wild falcon, lacking the assistance of the falconer, is at real risk of injury if it hunts gulls. A gull certainly does not seem to have the same appeal to the young hawk that a pigeon or a partridge has.

Anyway, once the tyro is confident binding to the smaller gulls, larger gulls can be used. I allow her plenty of time on the carcass, letting her plume it at her leisure and always assisting her by wiping away the annoying small, downy feathers that adhere to her beak, nares, and eyes. I let her take her pleasure on the head and neck before feeding her the rest of the day's ration of day-old-chicks on the fist. Incidentally, some of the old books describe gull flesh as unpalatable to hawks and advise against feeding up on the stricken gull. I have to say that I have never found this to be the case. Admittedly a seasoned gull-hawk in high condition in an aviary will often ignore a gull carcass dropped in during the morning until later in the day when she realises that it's all there is on offer – no chicks today. Likewise a merlin that only a few weeks previously would have flown into the heavens in pursuit of a lark will now sit looking nonplussed (if a hawk can show such an expression) when its natural prey is dropped into the aviary. *Son of Hellboy*, the jerkin, will tuck into his conquered gull with gusto but if I produce a chick in the glove he will be on the fist without me having to bend down – it's just a question of taste. The majority of us humans would much rather eat a bar of chocolate than a floret of broccoli, but wouldn't want the chocolate if set beside a salmon fillet. The flesh of gulls is dark and rich, care must be taken not to over-feed on it during the season or the hawk will get a little above herself.

When the young hawk is deemed ready to be entered, a suitable slip must be found. Assuming that the weather is fair, the ideal is a flock of not much more than fifty birds, some 50 to 100 yards upwind (though the wind should be light), and well away from any water. Making sure there are no rooks or crows in the vicinity is something easier said than done. It's astonishing that a hawk trained on a white lure and dead gulls, and that has never seen anything black in its life, will totally ignore a flock of gulls and go hell for leather after the first crow it has ever seen. Unsuspecting gulls following the plough represent a good opportunity for a first slip. All that is required at this stage is for her to make a few kills. Herring and lesser black-backs are the gulls of choice. It shouldn't matter if there are small gulls present as the larger birds are slower to rise and offer easier targets, but steer clear of great black-backs. I once made this mistake with a young peregrine x saker which was proving a little troublesome to get started (the only consolation for any mistake made in falconry is that it acts as a learning curve. Anyone can make mistakes, but to repeat the same mistakes makes you a fool). This young hawk was slipped at a mixed flock of gulls and she ended up battling it out with a great black-back. I raced across the stubble to assist but by the time I arrived the hawk was face down with the gull on its back attempting to inflict serious damage with its powerful beak. So intent was it on killing the hawk that it either didn't notice my approach or didn't care and I was able to secure and kill it. The hawk was ruffled but had sustained no serious physical damage and I fed her up on the gull. Despite this, irreversible psychological damage had been done. I tried my best with her, but the hawk never so much as looked at another gull again.

No matter how diligent the training and entering process is, not all hawks will progress to becoming gull-hawks. A hawk may fit the bill physically but it also requires mental strength and a stout heart. A gull is a large and aggressive quarry and not all hawks have the bottle to face one. With any luck, all will go to plan and the hawk will be entered and make a good start. All that the tyro requires at this early stage is to get some gulls under her belt, gain confidence, and become wedded to her quarry. Only when this has been achieved can we turn our attention to the quality of the flights. If the hawk should take a crow, or any other form of check, it should be removed from her as promptly as possible and before she has had a chance to break into it. Of course not even a beak-full of food should be allowed her as you pick her up. She should be hooded and tried again later in the day or, failing that, next morning. Sticking stringently to this rule will make the hawk learn the futility of taking a crow and realise there is nothing in it for her. Before long she will fly straight through a flock of corvids to get to a gull without being tempted in the slightest to check.

On the land over which I fly there is always water in the distance. What seems a hell of a long way to me evidently doesn't look that way to a hunted gull that can see possible sanctuary in far-off water. This may be a reason for the lower percentage of true high flights than may be achieved by a falconer flying over perfect country. It may be possible to increase the percentage of high flights by flying a cast, when the lesser of the two hawks chases the gull well up before the better hawk is slipped, much in the manner used in lark-hawking with a cast of merlins. I have had the classic ringing *haut vol* when gull-hawking but it has to be said that it is not a common occurrence, even when slipping at gulls on passage. Even common gulls will ring immediately after evading a stoop but will then level out and never seem to want to reach for the clouds. It is no guarantee of high flights to fly at gulls on passage. More often than not the flight just ends further away and turns into a tracking session. The majority of the time the gulls seem content with trying to out fly the hawk whilst heading in the direction of some distant water. It is surprising just how agile the larger gulls are when being hard pressed, especially in the windy conditions of which they are masters.

The majority of decent flights at gulls can be compared to the high mounting flights to be seen in lark-hawking, but they are longer and, arguably perhaps, more exciting because the gulls are not looking to bail for cover, while the lark, once it loses its confidence in its ability to outfly the hawk has only one objective in mind. Even where no cover seems to be available the lark will try to use the sparsest tussock of grass, a flock of sheep, or the falconer's legs and the flight will be spoiled. This seeking of strange cover reminds me of the time I slipped a musket out of the window of the Landrover at some starlings thirty yards away in the middle of an open field. As the hawk closed in on his chosen bird it dropped to the ground and the musket overshot. The starling doubled back and headed straight for the vehicle. It flew through the open window and hid in the dash!

Just a word on sparrowhawk behaviour. I quote from the great artist naturalist and OHC member of the 19th and 20th century, George Lodge:

> *The sparrowhawk is credited by some people with occasionally having the habit of disguising its manner of flight with the object of so deceiving its prospective prey as to allow a close approach. This style of flight, which I have never seen myself, is described as being executed in a slow and rolling manner, quite different from its usual dashing and gliding. I have never heard of anyone describing a kill from such tactics, and it may be doubted whether there is any foundation for the belief, even if the fact of this style of flight be granted. There is too much of this crediting animals with a human type of intelligence on slender anecdotal evidence.*

I was once crossing an open extent of ploughed ground, sparrowhawk on fist. There was a small flock of starlings some hundred plus yards away, so I unhooded the hawk to see what she made of them. After a second or two to weigh up the situation she dropped vertically from the fist like a stone, just opening her wings before she hit the ground. She then flew towards the starlings with a slow rowing kind of wingbeat, not dissimilar to a lapwing. Initially the starlings seemed unconcerned, bringing her much closer than ordinarily would have been possible, before adopting the usual sparrowhawk dash. She failed to kill I might add.

After which digression I shall get back to my subject of gulls in front of a hawk …

Like great black-backs, albeit to a lesser extent, herring and lesser black-backed gulls are not generally used to having to fly for their lives from an aerial predator. Because of this, a hawked gull will often assume it is a victim of piracy and when hard-pressed will regurgitate the food in its crop. An experienced gull-hawk will ignore this action but on several occasions I have had a hawk break off from the flight and drop down to the discarded food before realising its mistake. It is not a new phenomenon; the same thing occasionally happened at Didlington and Loo in the grand old days of heron-hawking.

Of the commoner British species of gull the black-headed is by far the hardest to catch. I catch a few each season but am always suspicious and give each one a thorough checking over to ascertain its condition. A hawk has to be fully fit, agile, and persevering to take one in fair flight and if other gulls are present the hawk will almost always go for the easier target. In view of this, if wanting to specialise in black-heads, it would be better to use smaller hawks that would be physically incapable of taking the larger species and therefore less inclined to check. It would also be advisable to fly them in a cast. Tiercel barbaries or female 'perlins' might fit the bill. Greg is currently training a cast of peregrine x barbary falcons for the flight, good luck mate! The reason I don't follow St. Quintin and advocate a cast of tiercels is because the boldest of them will take the larger gulls, as did *Sicknote*, the last tiercel I flew out of the hood. (He also took a heron!)

In 1889 W H St Quintin's hawks killed 49 gulls in 88 flights, most of them with passage hawks flown in a cast. That only ten of the gulls taken were black-headed shows just what a difficult quarry they are.

A dog is not necessary for gull-hawking but, seeing that my dog is largely redundant come the end of the lark-hawking season I like to take her along to enjoy the sport. At times she does come in useful in helping to flush a gull that has made it to a small stretch of water. Another instance of her helping comes when the hawk has cut a gull down over water breaking a wing and she retrieves the injured quarry.

One last remark on the slip – never be tempted to fly at a loafing solitary gull. They are gregarious birds and one on its own may not be healthy and many succumb to botulism, particularly in late summer. I learnt this in Scotland when a single gull was all we could find. I slipped the hawk from a few hundred yards away, and the gull, an adult herring, remained motionless and waited to die!

On the type of land that I fly over, gull-hawking has shown a consistently better quality of sport than rook- or crow-hawking. A far higher percentage of flights remain in full view (the whole point of falconry) with far fewer descending into rat-hunts. Access to land for gull-hawking can be a little problematic. In truth when slipping from a roadside or similar no permission is needed from anyone. The gulls don't belong to anyone, neither does the air space – something about which the law has concurred with me. If and when the hawk comes down with a gull, on whoever's land, it is my property and I am entitled to retrieve it. But don't get me wrong; I am not advocating that you should go off gull-hawking wherever and whenever you like. In the areas where I hawk I make every effort to make myself known to as many famers and landowners as I can, informing them of my activities and intentions, seeking their blessing, and keeping everything as cordial as possible. The majority of the people I approach seem quite relaxed and agreeable to the proceedings, especially when I point out that the hawk will neither catch game-birds nor frighten them off the land (referring to the survey done by the Game Conservancy some years ago), but some take more convincing than others about this. However, with the flight capable of covering several miles in any direction, especially in a strong wind, you can still find yourself in unfamiliar territory. In such situations my first thought is to secure the hawk before she can come to any possible harm. Then, if there are any farmers or workers in the vicinity, I will approach them, apologise for being on the land and explain the situation. With any luck I will have secured another area of land free from hostility. I keep well clear of keepered land if I can, but generally such places are anyway less conducive to gull-hawking. Gamekeepers tend to be less tolerant of hawks (and falconers) – full stop.

When lark-hawking I fly over public-access moorland, but still take care to liaise with any individuals who also hawk there or hold the sporting rights.

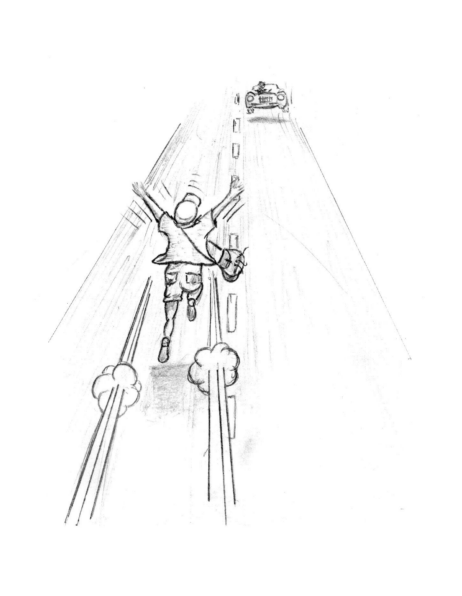

CHAPTER THREE

It's Dangerous Out There!

"Lost my knife, my luncheon and my temper. Broke two lure strings and lamed my horse badly, what fun it is to be Hon. Sec. to a Grand Old Hawking Club!"

Gerald Lascelles, March 26th 1884

BEFORE UNHOODING AND slipping the hawk there are so many factors to be taken into consideration: wind speed and direction; the weather in general; position of the quarry; anticipated behaviour of the quarry; the direction in which it will fly; whether it will be downwind; the availability of cover; and the presence of check that may tempt the hawk. Extra care is needed in the case of a young hawk that may not have learnt its vocation in life. All this assumes that your hawk is fit and in prime condition for the flight. Despite every precaution being taken, one cannot legislate for every eventuality: things can, and sometimes do, go wrong. Your fate may be in the lap of the gods with flights out of the hood; your hawk may come down with her quarry almost anywhere in this vastly overcrowded island of ours but a lot of grief can be avoided by carefully choosing when (and when not) to take the slip.

Long flights, or ones where the quarry has not behaved as it was 'supposed to', can easily end over built-up areas. Then, when the hawk binds to gull or corvid and all that is visible is buildings, it is heart-in-the-mouth time. Is she on a road? Will she be run over? Are people going to interfere with her? Is she in a garden? Are there any dogs about? or cats? On several occasions I have ended up in someone's back garden, and the majority of times there has been no-one at home. Then it's just a case of sorting the hawk out and making a sharp exit, though I do wonder quite what the occupants, when they return home, will make of the pile of feathers on their lawn (or, on one occasion, on the tennis-court in the grounds of a country mansion). On the few occasions when the inhabitants have been in residence I have, surprisingly enough, met with little hostility. Indeed I can recall one pleasant afternoon in North Yorkshire, when I sat at a patio-table drinking tea with the lady owner of the isolated cottage whilst we watched *Sachin*, my peregrine, feeding upon her rook on the lawn (and no, we didn't get any further than sharing tea and conversation). It was over the same ground that *Sachin* flew her rook in the opposite direction, towards the village a couple of miles away. I tracked her down to a new housing complex on its outskirts where she was on an area of grass against the side wall of a house, contentedly consuming her rook, oblivious of the semi-circle of onlookers gathered around her. *"Let me through, please. I'm a doctor."* A situation of the opposite kind once met a fellow merlin-man. He received stinging rebuke from the owner of another isolated cottage, into the garden of which the hard-pressed lark had bailed for cover and been taken by the hawk. The man was shaking with rage and holding in his hand the body of the "poor lark" that he had taken from the merlin. If it had been my merlin that he robbed, his rage might have been reciprocated.

Triple Trouble, a peregrine x gyr x saker of the fine line produced by Ray Turner, once bound to an adult lesser black-back after a very fine flight, but came down over a small, rough, South Yorkshire town. By the time I arrived I was more than a little concerned over the nature of the surroundings – several people in the vicinity and dangerous-looking dogs wandering around. In the midst of this concrete jungle I found a small oasis of a bowling green surrounded by a six-foot fence with a locked gate. There sat *Triple* happily pluming her gull. On another occasion with *Triple* she didn't reach *terra firma*, coming down with her gull on a warehouse roof in an industrial estate. Fortunately the staff were most helpful and managed to get me out on the roof via a combination of lift, staircase, and hatch door. That was not quite the case when a similar situation arose in Berkshire with *Sicknote*, the tiercel, on a roof-top with his rook. No way were the Security going to allow me up there – Health and Safety and all that. I did my best to explain the situation and the implications: at best the tiercel could be out for a night, at worst lost for good – all to no avail. Oh well, I had tried the polite approach. Now was the time to tell them, in no uncertain terms, that I was going up there anyway to retrieve my hawk: "Right, mate. You can either unlock the gate for me so that I can take the outside stairs or else I'll scale the outside of the building. It's up to you." He chose the former.

Some hawks can take matters a stage further. Whilst flying a sparrowhawk in Dalton, Nick and I lost sight of her as she flipped over a hedge. We searched high and low but found no trace whatever. No telemetry... Subsequently a chap from the garage at the end of the lane asked us if we had lost a hawk because one had chased a bird into his house above the garage through an open door and was then enjoying her meal on his living-room carpet.

A similar incident with a shortwing was arguably the strangest of them all, and very likely unique. On a glorious late January morning I set out with my goshawk in eager anticipation of some good sport. I didn't have to go far – out of my back garden, over a field with public access, and into the surrounding countryside which held enough rabbits and gamebirds to keep me going throughout the season. Set in that green and pleasant land is a prison, HMP Full Sutton, Category A. The prison has an area of short grass stretching out 30 yards from the perimeter wall and then a strip of copse running right round its outskirts. *Gemma*, my English springer spaniel bitch, soon flushed a cock pheasant and the gos was away. The pheasant rose steeply out of the trees, closely pursued. Both birds topped the prison wall and headed over the prison, which is of rectangular shape, with the quarry cutting the corner and heading for the copse on the other side. I made my way round, expecting to find the gos either on her kill or taking stand in the trees where the pheasant had put in. She wasn't in the trees and after a thorough search was not to be found in the undergrowth – again no telemetry! Then a pair of carrion crows started to circle, and call angrily, indicating to me, I was pretty sure,

35

the whereabouts of the hawk on her kill. The only problem was that they were circling over the other side of the prison wall. Blagging your way into gardens and on to buildings is one thing, but talking your way into a maximum security prison is quite another. When I went to the main gate to explain the situation one thing soon became clear – I was not going in! I was able to explain roughly where I thought the hawk was and the guards looked on the CCTV but found no sign. One of them said he could send a couple of prison officers round (with dogs!) to have a look, but that wouldn't be for half an hour as the prisoners were out on exercise. The thought of my gos on her pheasant with murderers and terrorists wandering around did little to lighten my mood. Then I remembered Dave. He lived locally, had flown a few hawks, and worked for the prison. It was a Saturday, and Dave was off work, but the guards and I managed to get hold of him and he was only too glad to help. I gave him my glove and then sat down in the manner of an expectant father. Was she all right? Had she shredded herself on the razor wire? Had she been frightened off her quarry by the convicts, or even killed? After what seemed like an age Dave returned, on his fist a goshawk sporting a crop that couldn't possibly have held another morsel. His drinks were on me down in the village that evening.

As well as buildings and inhabited areas, Britain's vast network of roads and railways forms another potential hazard, while in more remote parts of the country, even lanes, farm tracks, and public footpaths can spell trouble where flying out of the hood is concerned. My worst disaster from traffic, although not when flying out of the hood, came when a promising young goshawk strayed too close to a railway line and was cut down in her prime by a passing 125. It could have been worse, I suppose. I almost met the same fate as I wandered along the track picking up pieces of goshawk.

A slight digression, but just an observation on modern Britain. I'm so glad I no longer fly goshawks, how do austringers cope these days? Everywhere I go there seems to be chickens wandering about the countryside. They are chickens for Christ's sake; they eat, shit and lay eggs. I doubt they have the brain capacity to worry about their environment.

When it comes to roads I have had more good luck than bad to be fair, though I could do without the stress of the close calls. *Sachin*, previously mentioned, was twice tracked down on her quarry to within feet of the hard shoulder of a busy motorway. Likewise, in the North-West, *Triple Trouble* twice came down with her gull far too close to the M66 for comfort. One of the merlin-men was not so fortunate when his jack met a lorry when attempting to cross the M25 and lay dead by the central reservation from where he could not be retrieved. You may be surprised to hear this but apparently pedestrians are not allowed on the motorway, and neither are the Sri Lankan Cycling Team! *Sachin* again, this time in Hampshire, took her rook on the opposite side of the M27. It was late afternoon and my first thought was to secure the hawk, just as any falconer would. I had just made it across six lanes when I saw the police-car approaching. I was scrambling up the bank through the saplings when the car pulled up. *"Oi! Come here!"* For a few seconds I considered carrying on running but that would almost certainly result in an arrest if I was caught and *Sachin* would, at best, be out for the night. I approached the two officers sheepishly. One of them was an attractive WPC (whose telephone number I failed to obtain by the way). *"What the hell were you doing? Don't you know you're not allowed on the motorway?"* "I'm terribly sorry," I replied. "I'm not from around here. I thought it was an A road." When I explained the situation they were genuinely interested and gave me a lift to within a couple of hundred yards of the signal. I apologised again and thanked them sincerely for their help (Still no telephone number. To be honest I think I might have had more chance with the PC. Or am I being facetious?). *"Now, you're not going to attempt to go back over the motorway, are you?"* he said. As if I would!

Sachin again, this time in Berkshire. She flew her rook into the distance and out of sight. As I homed in on the signal down a quiet country lane I spotted her with her rook on the edge of the tarmac a couple of hundred yards ahead. At that precise moment a four-wheel-drive vehicle came out of a side road and turned left, heading in the direction of the hawk. It was only a narrow lane and there didn't seem to be enough room for the vehicle to pass her safely. Would the driver see the hawk and avoid her? Or would he deliberately try to run her over? Or, like the majority of the general public, not see her at all? There was nothing I could do except look on. By pure good fortune, the wheels missed her by inches as she unconcernedly continued with her meal.

Whilst flying *Casper*, one of Nick's fine merlins, and an exceptional one at that, a fine ringing flight developed. The lark shot skywards and *Casper* set off downwind before powering back upwind, gaining height, before both birds began to ring. This was on Moss Moor, over the Pennines, with the dreaded M62 well in the distance. Up and up the flight went, drifting on the breeze, until before long the birds were out of sight. The signal grew weaker – and finally was lost. There followed a long haul over the moor towards the motorway until the signal could be picked up again. It was heading for the traffic. At Junction 22 there is a small triangular copse splitting the slip-road from the motorway. In its thick undergrowth sat a contented *Casper*, with a bulging crop and surrounded by lark feathers.

Incidentally, I had Nick's son Peter's notorious English setter with me, *Chaos*, or *No Brain* as he was frequently called. *Chaos* couldn't negotiate the sheep-fence at the edge of the moor and sat there howling while I was picking the merlin up. As I made my way back I saw a car pull up on the slip-road and a woman get out because she thought the dog was lost. When, later, I told Nick, he said I should have hidden in the cover and let her take him! Earlier in that season I had taken *Chaos* to Richard's moor near Accrington. He made no comment throughout the hawking but, back at the vehicles at the end of the evening, and without warning, Richard suddenly said, *"That's the worst dog I've ever seen on this moor."* I think Nick had the right idea!

Up in Yorkshire *KP*, a peregrine x saker hybrid, came down with her gull about a mile away, near a country lane, and from where son Thomas and I were watching it looked too close for comfort. We knew we were right when we saw a car pull up. What were the intentions of the occupants? We jumped in the van and raced round. There was *KP* still in the process of subduing a large herring gull, and being watched with interest by a young couple and small son all peering out of the car windows. *KP* had survived a closer call in the previous season when I had slipped her at a small flock of herring gulls to the west of York. Unfortunately the gulls didn't react as expected and turned downwind. *KP* singled out her gull and flew it into the distance until over the built-up area of Acomb. Fortunately, after surviving a stoop, the gull turned upwind and headed in my direction. Eventually *KP* clipped the gull and bound to it on the next stoop, coming down with it not fifty yards from where I stood. Perfect, I thought, but as they hit the ground the gull broke free and the chase was resumed – with both birds heading for the York ring-road. They disappeared from view as they went over the hedge running parallel to the road. Shit! I ran at my best pace and on making it to the road could see *KP* with her gull some two hundred yards away close to the white line in the centre of the road, with traffic speeding past on either side of her. I ran towards her, in the middle of the road, waving my arms frantically in an attempt to stop the traffic. Passing motorists were looking at me as if I'd just escaped from an asylum. As I was getting nearer to the hawk a car on my left slowed down and a white van coming in the opposite direction stopped, allowing me to pick up hawk and gull and put them down on the verge. Phew! I waved apologetically.

A&E

Others have not been so fortunate. Dave Taylor's fine gull-hawk, *Diamond*, now adorns his living-room wall after being hit by a car whilst on her gull up in Scotland.

Even while well away from the dangers of the travel networks there are still plenty of hazards out there. At Wintringham, over near the East Coast, I was flying *Cally*, (named after the Highland football team in the region she was entered), a peregrine x saker hybrid and one of the finest gull-hawks I have seen, let alone owned. A superb flight at a common gull ended from my perspective with both birds disappearing in the direction of the Humber. I arrived, not far from the estuary where doubtless the gull had found sanctuary, to find the hawk stone dead at the base of a telegraph pole, having been electrocuted. The following season another hawk, this one belonging to Dave Taylor, suffered a similar fate.

On a fine September evening I was out trying to enter *Oyster*, my female perlin. She had put a small covey of English partridges into a hedge and continued to wait on while *Fudge*, the GSP, and I tried our best to manufacture the re-flush that would send the partridges across the open field. This we failed to do and they broke down the hedgerow. *Oyster* stooped; there was a puff of feathers and no throw-up. I sauntered to the spot with a feeling of satisfaction that the objective had been achieved. I arrived at the partridge feathers and peered into the ditch. There lay *Oyster*, on her back, dead. The partridge feathers lay on both sides of a sheep-fence. I assumed that this was what she had hit, breaking her neck. There was, by the way, no sign of the partridge. The action had seemed so innocuous, especially after seeing a peregrine slam into a Scottish deer-fence in pursuit of her grouse and looking as if she had decapitated herself, only for it to prove nothing worse than being slightly winded.

There seemed nothing untoward when *Sachin* stooped to take her crow just before it would have reached cover. I went to pick her up from where she was, twenty yards from the hedge that the crow had been making for. She was right next to a single-wire fence. This she must have hit, since, as I tried to get her on to the fist, her right leg hung limply, but I couldn't feel a break. To this day I still cannot remember why I chose, or what possessed me, to take her to the local vet instead of taking her up to Mr Nigel Harcourt-Brown. The X-ray showed tendon-damage which the vet said he could do nothing with. His advice to have her put down was politely declined. I flew her next day to help with her circulation and to give her good foot some respite. She killed a crow. Having only one foot didn't matter to *Sachin*! A fortnight later and the leg was as good as new – clearly just a sprain. Since then I have never taken an injured hawk to anyone other than Mr Harcourt-Brown, nor will I ever again.

More recently *KP* was up and down at a gull as the flight went out of sight. A few minutes later she came back in to the lure but her leg was hanging down and, as I subsequently found out, badly dislocated. I don't know whether she had hit a fence or something similar as she was driving the gull down or whether she had hit the gull at the wrong angle (though I think that is unlikely for such an experienced hawk). Anyway, it was up to Harrogate where it was touch and go whether the operation to repair the leg would be successful or whether she would have to be put down. The news from Nigel next day was that he wasn't entirely happy with the position of the leg and so he operated a second time. She was kept up at Harrogate as the next 48 hours were vital for the leg to be kept in place and to stay there. Which, much to Nigel's and my delight, it did. After the two days I picked her up, but we weren't out of the woods yet. She still had to be kept quiet for another three weeks to give the joint time to strengthen. To achieve this I kept her loose in the mews on a low perch from which she could lie down if she needed to. She was kept hooded and only unhooded each day to be fed. When the time came to head back to Nigel's again, another X-ray showed the leg to be in perfect condition although she was still using it a little gingerly and movement was a bit restricted. Although pleased with her progress Nigel said the acid test would come when she started hunting again. Would the leg stand up to the rigours of taking large gulls? Another three weeks later and after a couple of weeks of fitness work to the lure, *KP* was back in the groove. Top job, Nigel – Top Man.

On another occasion *Hellboy* the jerkin was putting in repeated stoops at an adult lesser black-back. So intent was the gull on watching the hawk and avoiding his stoops that it flew into a telephone wire, slicing a wing clean off. It's a sobering thought that this could just as easily have happened to the hawk.

Vermin and the like

a) At home

As well as inanimate objects to collide with, there are plenty of threats from living creatures. The list of them goes on and on.

Before the hawk has even entered the field, consideration has to be given to the seemingly innocuous and peaceful environment of the garden. First and foremost hazard – vermin. Aviaries, weathering ground, and mews must all be fox-proof. There have been instances of them tunnelling in at night and taking the occupants. Rats should be dealt with as a matter of course, not just because of the usual problems they cause but also because, perhaps surprisingly, they can pose a direct threat to the hawks themselves. The last sparrowhawk I flew was killed by rats in the mews at the end of her first season. I was aware rats were living under my garden shed and my wife was on at me to sort them out. Regrettably, I procrastinated and paid the price. From my investigation it appeared that *Rattus norvegicus* and friends had come along the screen-perch, causing the hawk to bate and a bite to the head is what killed her. After that they had eaten away her back.

Cats are top of the vermin list and should not be tolerated in the slightest. After the long haul from Yorkshire to Cornwall to visit my parents I wanted to weather *KP* on the lawn. I quizzed them about their pet cat and was told it was out and about somewhere but they assured me it never took the slightest interest in birds. I put her on her block and retired into the house. No sooner had I done so than *Tiddles* appeared from the shrubbery, raced across the lawn, and leapt on the hawk in the manner of a lion taking a wildebeest. We are talking about a large peregrine x saker here, and *Tiddles* was lucky he belonged to my parents – otherwise he would be 'pushing up the daisies'. *KP* has never forgotten the incident and even now the slightest glimpse of a cat will send her into a frantic bate.

There is also the increasing possibility of aerial attack. I heard recently of a wild buzzard attacking a peregrine out on the block and then being joined by a second buzzard.

A falconer went to work leaving his tiercel on the block. He returned to be met by the sight of a hybrid falcon standing contentedly on the block having killed and eaten his tiercel. It was a lost hawk, of course.

This incident leads me to a rather disturbing modern phenomenon. The countryside seems to be awash with 'feral' Harris hawks. The cheap availability of these birds, and the ease with which they can be trained, has led to all manner of unskilled people acquiring them, either as pets to impress their mates or by a would-be falconer lacking the required knowledge. There are reports that Harris hawks are even breeding with wild buzzards. This whole situation can only lead to grave repercussions, at best bringing the grand old sport into disrepute, at worst hastening the day that the powers that be ban falconry altogether.

Only recently Chris was flying his tiercel at snipe, the hawk missing in the stoop, chasing his quarry out of sight. Chris tracked his hawk down to a small copse, the hawk having taken its quarry, only to be confronted with the sight of a large female Harris hawk on top of his tiercel. Obviously Chris acted with haste and fortunately his hawk survived the ordeal and made a full recovery. Chris subsequently found out that the Harris hawk had belonged to a chap who formerly kept budgerigars and when the last of these died decided to get a bird of prey. The first one he obtained died, the second escaped from the aviary.

Richard even had his merlin attacked by a woodpigeon that was 'protecting' its young.

Although not exactly an aerial threat, birds such as guinea fowl and peacocks are a lethal threat to any weathering hawk or falcon.

I never leave small hawks weathering unattended and even when in my presence I like the dogs to be in the garden. After all if you are in the house it only takes a few seconds for disaster to strike while you are otherwise engaged. Similarly with large hawks I will weather them in the open only in the presence of a dog or dogs. Even then don't assume that this is foolproof. I once put out a peregrine to weather and bathe while I returned to the house. Shortly afterwards I heard the hawk obviously in distress. I ran into the garden to find that in the act of bathing somewhat vigorously she had put her head down in the water and managed to get it under her leash and was in the process of strangling herself.

b) In the field

I was once sitting daydreaming as my musket was feeding up on a starling he had taken. My friend then turned up and asked if I hadn't noticed the large ginger cat stalking my hawk!

A merlin I was flying on an airfield took a lark and put down in a cabbage-field on the outskirts. I walked towards the spot and when I was within 100 yards a fox appeared out of the cover, merlin in mouth and trotted casually away. A postscript to that story is that I bought another bull x greyhound lurcher intending to exact some sort of revenge on *Reynard*. I don't know if we killed that particular fox, but the chance of it made me feel a lot better. My friend Warren suffered a similar loss when a fox killed his excellent tiercel on a rook it had just taken.

Wild peregrines and ravens can be a nuisance during lark-hawking, but interference from buzzards can be fatal. It is a long time since Steve Benjamin had his merlin, with her last lark in her feet, killed by one on Dartmoor that came down on her within view of the field. It is only too recently that my merlin, *Nasri*, suffered the same fate in a distant plantation after taking a lark – but more of that later.

Only recently Rodney was weathering his jack merlin, when the phone rang. In the short time it took to answer the telephone his hawk had been killed by a buzzard.

Whilst flying *KP* at gulls in Cornwall, the flight had gone out of sight and she failed to return. Tracking the hawk, I was almost upon her, expecting to find her on her gull at any moment when the signal grew faint – she was on the wing. I eventually recovered her just before dusk as she came into the lure, a wild falcon wheeling overhead, her face was covered in blood from a cut on her cere and she had a bruised left foot. More light was shed on proceedings the following day when she cast up a good size, gull-feathered casting. So she had taken her gull. Had the wild peregrine stooped at her and raked her, or had they grappled on the ground? Or was the peregrine just a coincidence and a buzzard had come and robbed her?

Hawks sometimes come down with their quarry amongst livestock. Sheep tend to be startled and decide that discretion is the better part of valour and bolt. On the other hand cattle are inquisitive and will form a circle round hawk and quarry but usually keep their distance.

Horses are excitable and unpredictable (and a bloody pain on Bodmin). I was once flying a goshawk that put his quarry in and took stand near the river Derwent. Before I had a chance to call him back half a dozen horses came galloping along, sending him across the river with alacrity. He would not return to the fist, not even to the dead lure, owing to the presence of the horses which I had failed to drive away. Daylight was running out. I calculated that there was not enough time to go all the way back to the van, drive to the nearest bridge, and reach the hawk before dark. There was only one course of action to take. Now swimming across the swollen river Derwent in mid-winter, wearing Barbour, wellies, and all, followed by a two hour walk back to the van is not to be recommended. All's well that ends well though.

Hazards

Water is a familiar problem to a gull-hawker, but presents a different one when in the form of ice. Proper winter weather seems to be a rarity these days but we do sometimes still get a week or two of hard frost, and then gull-holding areas that are usually unsuitable due to the presence of water suddenly look inviting when lakes and ponds are frozen over. Yet gulls that are flown at these times are reluctant to stray far from the frozen water, still looking upon it as a sanctuary. Most hawks on the other hand do not view the ice as anything other than solid ground and the gull as fair game anywhere (although *KP* will still not go for gulls over frozen water). I have gone through ice a few times when retrieving hawk and quarry from small areas of frozen water, but fortunately have ended up no more than chest deep. Two other occasions spring to mind which could have had (literally) graver consequences.

A young ¾ peregrine / ¼ gyr had a fine flight at an adult lesser black-back, her best flight to date. As she was stooping at the gull the flight went out of sight over the brow of a hill where I knew there was a lake, but frozen in the sub-zero temperatures of that time. On reaching the brow I was greeted by the sight of a black mass of corvids in the centre of the frozen lake attacking the hawk on her quarry. I ran down at my best pace, shouting and waving my arms, and eventually dispersing the corvids when I reached the edge of the lake. Now for the next problem. Normally in that situation I would be tying a dead lure to the creance and throwing it out next to the hawk in hope she

would transfer from one gull to the other and then I could gently reel her in. But this hawk was too far out to throw a gull anywhere near her, and the lake was too large, with too much cover round the edge to trail the line round to the other side and drag the dead lure across to her. Apart from that I didn't actually have a dead lure with me. I put the receiver down, my mobile phone between my teeth, and cautiously set forth over the ice. I soon reached the point of no return, no man's land. If the ice was to give then, so be it – there was nothing I could do about it. The silence was only broken by the creaking of the ice under my weight. The further I went out the louder it seemed to get but the ice held! I made it out to the hawk, and, mightily relieved, back to terra firma. Nobody in their right mind, apart from a falconer whose over-riding thought is to secure his hawk would contemplate such actions.

On the other occasion, when I tracked *Triple* with her gull down to the centre of a frozen lake, the problem was exacerbated by the fact it was in a public park. Three elderly gentlemen with their dogs were at the edge of the ice watching the hawk. As I approached: *"Is that yours?"* from one of them. "Yes. It is," as I took a couple of layers off. *"You're not going out there, are you? I wouldn't if I were you. The ice won't hold you."* "Yes, I am," I declared. The three of them were joined by three more people, with two cars pulling up at the roadside, no doubt not wanting to miss seeing this idiot drop through the ice without much chance of a rescue. The ice was creaking and as I neared the hawk it also began to crack. I lay down to spread my weight and commando-crawled towards her. *Triple* took exception to my strange approach and stepped back off the gull. I took hold of it and slid gently back until I reached the bank, with *Triple* still standing on the ice. I politely cleared the onlookers back and threw the gull down on the bank where it was gratefully accepted by the hawk.

It is not only shortwings that have a habit of making kills in inaccessible places. On more than one occasion I have had to climb a tree or scale a tall thorny bush where a longwing has taken a rook or crow as it put in, but once, when out on open moorland in Cornwall, *Flappy* the merlin had a ringing flight that drifted off the moor with the wind and when they were over a conifer plantation the hard-pressed lark bailed for cover. I made my way down off the moor to the edge of the woodland. A strong signal indicated I was right on her but I couldn't see her anywhere until I looked up and saw her in the upper branches of a larch tree looking a little uncomfortable as she plumed her lark. I put the receiver down, removed my hat, and started to climb. When I got up there the hawk was nowhere to be seen. I thought I must have spooked her whilst climbing and she had carried her lark down to a more comfortable and peaceful spot. I climbed down, picked up the receiver, and found the signal was exactly the same. I looked up and saw she was still there. I had climbed the wrong tree! Anyway, second time lucky, although a descent with hawk on fist is always a little tricky.

As well as difficulties and dangers from outside influences there are also the actions of the hawk itself, deliberate or otherwise, that lead to trouble.

A goshawk of mine had a tendon severed by a squirrel – no doubt a fairly common occurrence amongst austringers who regularly fly tree-rats – though this time the injury was successfully operated on. Another goshawk broke a wing in tackling a brown hare, a bad break that she never fully recovered from.

Large gulls are a formidable quarry and can easily inflict injury if the hawk has a poor hold. They will grip a hawk's wing with their powerful beak and twist their heads in an attempt to break a bone. On more than one occasion I have had to rest a hawk for a few weeks with a badly bruised wing. The worst of these was *Skye*, a peregrine x saker hybrid who was laid up for six weeks after a battle with a great black-back (as I've explained before, it's not a quarry that I fly intentionally these days). *Skye* was not averse to tackling large quarry; geese, black-backed and glaucous gulls, but was terrified of other birds of prey – and herons! I have twice seen her robbed of her quarry by common buzzards, but her greatest fear was of red kites. The merest sight of one would send her screaming in alarm towards the horizon. She was once lost for twelve days following such an incident. In contrast, I once tracked down *KP* on her gull to find her contentedly eating her meal with three kites standing patiently around her in a perfect triangle. My kingdom for a camera!

As well as the intended quarry, hawks can be inclined to check at unsuitable quarry, especially young and inexperienced ones. Some hawks apparently can't resist the increasingly common, common buzzard. This has only happened once for me when a young peregrine was slipped at gulls on passage in the Highlands. She gained height, flew straight through the gulls, and pulled down an unsuspecting buteo. In instances such as this, no time should be wasted in making in before the buzzard has had a chance to inflict any form of injury.

A sparrowhawk of mine once caught a long-eared owl, though when

I made in it was difficult to tell who had caught whom – although it was not quite such a commotion as when my redtail smashed into a patch of nettles and grabbed a large black cat.

Corvids will often mob a hawk that is hunting, which can be off-putting to an inexperienced gull-hawk and result in a spoilt flight. They can also be a dangerous quarry when downed, quite apart from the angry mob that piles in to assist their captured brethren, as the following will testify. *Black Dwarf*, a very small dark peregrine (the clue is in the name!) had only recently been entered on corvids with only a few head to her name. On this particular day she had taken her crow on the other side of a narrow river, and on making my way hastily to the water I was able to disperse the mobbing flock from my side. Immediate danger over, I made my way in no great hurry to the nearest bridge. On approaching I could hear the crow and was surprised and a little perturbed that it was still alive. I arrived to find the crow on its back and both birds having hold of the other's legs. The crow was free to use his beak, and had done so, blinding the hawk in the left eye.

Sicknote was another of Nick Wilkinson's excellent hawks. The tiercel acquired his title due to a string of ailments and injuries. He nearly died during training from a bad bout of 'cocci' before I had discovered Appertex and begun to deliver these 'magic bullets' immediately to all new hawks and at regular intervals thereafter. In his first few weeks in the field he seemed to suffer one minor injury after another. Anyway, when he was not long out of the moult, I was exercising him one fine summer's afternoon. He went up on the soar, so I delayed producing the lure and sat back to watch him. He drifted about half a mile away and, just as I was thinking of beginning his exercise, he put in a rattling vertical stoop from a vast height. No throw-up. He must have killed. By the time I reached him he was in a right mess – in fact I initially thought he was dead. He was on his back and the crow on top of him. It had broken into the flesh of both his legs, his right leg being by far the worst of them. I patched him up and put him on antibiotics. Just as I had treated *Sachin* after her leg injury, I decided to carry on flying him to aid his circulation. The following day I took him out to exercise him to the lure – and he killed a crow. *Sachin*esque! Although he went on to take many more corvids (as well as a heron!) over the next couple of seasons his right leg never fully recovered and he eventually succumbed to complications from the injury.

People

Last comes the arguably most dangerous hazard of them all, the planet's most numerous and dangerous vermin – humans.

I am not alone in having a hawk shot by an unknown 'sportsman,' (and would have had more if I hawked in France), nor in coming across a big man with a gun who threatens to shoot my hawk. My answer to his sort is always the same: "Well, you'd better save a cartridge for me because if you do shoot that hawk it will be the last thing you ever fucking do." In Scotland Kev Greensill's peregrine, a crow hawk, had put her quarry in and taken stand on a telegraph pole. Kev was some distance away when a car pulled up next to the pole. The driver went to the back of his car, took out a gun, and raised it to the hawk. Fortunately Kev's shouts alerted him and he calmly returned the gun to the boot and drove off. Trev Pick was tracking his crow-hawk, a peregrine x saker, which had killed some distance away, but as he closed in on her the banging signal suddenly stopped altogether. Almost simultaneously a Landrover sped away from the scene. *Triple Trouble* was either killed or stolen whilst on her gull, but more of that later.

Up in the Highlands again, *Cally*, the exceptional peregrine x saker hybrid, came down with her gull in a field where a tractor was harrowing. The tractor stopped and the driver got out and started walking towards her. Unsure of his intentions, I was racing across the field and shouting to try and attract his intention. As he came to the hawk he was raising his foot as if to stamp on her but at the last moment he was alerted by my shouting. I was too relieved that the hawk was unhurt to take umbrage about his conduct and so I approached apologetically for having had to enter his field to pick my hawk up. He was having none of it and ranted and raved about *"bloody 'awks. No wonder I've got no partridges,"* and *"that poor seagull. Look what it's doing to it!"* It obviously hadn't occurred to him that the numbers of large gulls in the area probably accounted for most of his partridge chicks. If he hadn't been such an old boy, the discussion would have been a much shorter one.

A similar situation arose to this one with *Triple Trouble*, when a walker appeared from a footpath and ran towards the hawk where she was controlling her gull. He was alerted by my shouting and stopped in his tracks a few yards away from hawk and gull. When I arrived I asked him what he had been doing. Initially he replied that he didn't know what he was seeing and was running over to take a look. Further conversation led to him claiming that he was sorry for the gull.

I worked on an ostrich-farm once, and was training a young peregrine on the land with the blessing of my boss. I had just given her the dead lure when the boss's father appeared in his four-wheel-drive, heading straight for the hawk. I was motionless. Time stood still. At the last moment the truck stopped just inches from the hawk. He got out and started ranting about how much he *"hated them bloody things"* and *"you're not to bring it on here again."* He was another one who could thank his age for not ending up on his backside.

I was once approached by a dog-walker when I was helping out *KP* with her gull. He was obviously spoiling for an argument. I asked him not to bring the dog any closer. He did just that, causing *KP* to leave her gull and take wing. Without going into further detail I think it's fair to say that this idiot will think twice before interfering with a falconer and his hawk again.

Another friend's hawk came down with her gull at the side of a road. When he arrived the gull was there but the hawk was not. Another motorist pulled over and told him that some lads had stopped, grabbed the hawk, and driven off. Later that day he got a telephone call from the thief (his number being on the flying jesses) demanding a ransom of £500 for the safe return of the hawk. The affair dragged on for a few days. The police were involved but, surprisingly, proved of little use. This story at least has a happy ending. Either the hawk escaped or was released by the thief when he realised he was not going to get any money. A few days later she was picked up, a little the worse for wear, but she made a full recovery.

In one of the areas of Yorkshire that I hawk in there is a landfill site, the reason the gulls are there in the first instance. If there are no gulls in the vicinity to provide a decent flight I will often go to the site to disperse the gulls there with a shotgun or similar device. In the past I did some part-time pest control there so that, still being on friendly terms with the staff and management, it can be somewhere to weather the hawks and socialise. On a fine Spring day I had been flying *Sicknote* in the area, and, as he had killed a rook and been fed up, I chose to put him on his block on the landfill site with a tiring rather than leaving him in the warm van, whilst Mick and I retired to The Sun for a pint. We were not gone long but on our return my heart sank when I was confronted by the sight of an empty block. My first thought was that he had been stolen, so I rang the police (what for I don't know. They were totally apathetic). However a closer inspection revealed the footprints in the soft grass where the offender had approached and on the opposite side of the block (*Sicknote* had obviously bated away from him) a few inches of leash were sunk into the ground where it had been cut through with a knife. Maybe this 'do-gooder' had thought he was being clever in "setting this poor bird free from its miserable existence," just too ignorant to realise he had almost certainly condemned the hawk to a slow death. I went up the bank to look across to the landfill site. Unusually, there were no birds on the site. I swung the lure and in he came, despite his full crop and still trailing two-thirds of his leash. Good job he was a greedy little bugger. I asked a lot of questions in search of the perpetrator but the only clue I got was that a contractor had come on site in my absence and had long since departed – back to Wales apparently. I guess he was feeling smug and pleased with himself, never imagining how lucky he was. This was the last time that I weathered hawks there. I should have known better. I had once left *Sachin* there for no more than ten minutes and come back to find her holding a cooked chicken leg (which fortunately she hadn't eaten). Generally speaking your average wagon-driver isn't necessarily the brightest spark in the fire.

On another occasion I had a hawk on the fist and a driver stopped me, took a piece of ham out of his sandwich, and handed it to me. "Thank you very much," I said as I ate it. The look of astonishment on his face was a picture as he replied, *that was for your bird!"*

Once when I had three hawks weathering on a landfill site I came back to find a neat ring of pieces of sandwich round each block, the perpetrator being meticulous in his efforts to make sure each hawk had its fair share. Give me strength!

It's easy to get to thinking that it's you against the world, but you do come across some decent and friendly people who restore your faith in human nature, albeit that their intentions may be misdirected or misconstrued.

Sicknote came down with a rook right on a public path and close to a terrier-man out with his dogs. He acted quickly to put the dogs on leads before they had a chance to snap the hawk up. On my arrival we had an agreeable conversation about falconry and field-sports in general.

I was tracking *Sachin* down in Berkshire when the signal grew weak and then disappeared altogether. It was late in the day and I searched until dusk and then drove round the area trying to pick up a signal but all to no avail. The following morning I received a telephone call from a chap (he had only just noticed the mobile phone number on the flying jesses) who said he had found my hawk the previous evening. My relief changed to anxiety when he explained that she was injured and had a lot of blood on her. When I arrived at his house very soon afterwards, he told me he had been out walking his dog and had come across *Sachin* on a rook. He dropped his coat over her, took her home, and put her in a black plastic dustbin inside his garden shed. It was with some trepidation that I opened the shed door, but there was *Sachin* perching contentedly on the lip of the bin with crop still bulging and none the worse for wear. The blood on her breast and tarsus came from the rook. Still, he received a nice bottle of malt for acting with the right and honourable intentions.

At RAF Elvington (no longer RAF) my merlin had a ringing flight at dusk that drifted out of sight towards the small industrial estate at the end of the airfield, now a much larger industrial estate that houses the Yorkshire Air Museum. I was led to a bus depot where the merlin was perched on top of a double-decker and a man was trying to reach up to the merlin with a long pole. I explained the situation and, as by then it was dark, called the hawk down in the artificial light of the depot. The man had mistaken the transmitter round her neck for some sort of dart and thought she had been shot.

In Lancashire, *KP* was slipped at gulls on passage and a stern chase developed that took her out of sight. She failed to return to the lure and I assumed she had killed. It was one of those situations where you have to weigh up your options and pick the best – would it be better to go back for the van or follow up on foot? Here experience comes into play, gauging how far away the hawk is from the signal received, whether she is down or still flying, considering the type of terrain that needs to be crossed, and checking whether there are rivers on the way. Obviously, if the signal is lost altogether, it's back to the vehicle and attach the roof aerial. On this occasion the signal was constant, if faint, and as I was sure she had killed I proceeded on foot. Up hill and down dale, across a couple of streams, and I ended up on a golf course, not far away from her by then.

A couple of green-keepers drove past in a golf-buggy and one of them asked me, without stopping, "have you lost a kestrel?" "No," said I, "something a bit bigger than that," thinking it was fairly astute of them when I consider I don't look much like a falconer, with no bag or vest and not wearing traditional country attire, although the receiver in my hand and the hood clipped to my pocket might give it away. I carried on walking and the signal became fainter. I did a 360° check and the signal was back where I'd just come from. How had I gone past her? As I retraced my steps I got a strong signal from the green-keepers' building but initially couldn't pinpoint it, until there it was – straight from the buggy the green-keepers had been driving. Shit! My first thought was that they had killed her and thrown her in the back of the buggy. Fearing the worst, I turned over a cardboard box, and there was *KP* with her gull, not wholly impressed with her treatment but otherwise fine. I sought out the green-keepers to ask them why they hadn't told me they that they had my hawk. They told me they hadn't realised it was my hawk and that I was looking for one! Ordinarily I would have suspected foul play and an attempt to get money from someone, but they had telephoned the number on the breeder's ring – not the more legible number on the flying jesses with REWARD written next to it. Talk about an IQ to match their shoe size!

My final word on encounters in the field relates to a group of people I have come across only recently – that is the 'twitchers' who gather to look at the gulls when word has got out that there is a rare migrant amongst the flock. As a keen ornithologist I can relate to this and will be interested to see the rare gull for myself. Relations with them are usually cordial and most take a keen interest in the hawk and enjoy watching the flight once I have made sure I am not spoiling their enjoyment by dispersing the gulls. There are also what I call the 'gull-gazers' who like to sit watching a flock of gulls all day, with no rarities present, and lack the specialist knowledge of the twitchers. They are the ones who take exception to my sport. One of them even threatened to get the landowner to shoot my jerkin. Some bird-lover! He was given short shrift. Only a short distance from where gulls gather on an airfield there is a public footpath through a wooded glade where there are, among others, tree-creepers, nuthatches, all three species of woodpecker, bullfinches, and long-tailed tits, all more interesting to me than a flock of gulls. Still, it would be a boring old world if we were all made the same.

Finally, to any aspiring falconer who after reading this chapter may want to give up before he has started, I can reassure him that the incidents described stretch over thirty-five years and most seasons pass without any major trials and tribulations.

Although I have stressed the care and consideration that need to be taken before a slip, there is a fine line between the over-cautious and the cavalier. There are no cast-iron guarantees when flying a hawk and if the falconer worries about every possible eventuality he will end up with a hawk that spends most of its days on the block and with himself lacking sport. He must harden his resolve, be willing to take a certain amount of risk and just 'get out there and do it' if quality flights are to be obtained.

Sachin

CHAPTER FOUR

The Hawks

A FEW NOTES on some of the hawks mentioned in the text:

Sachin: **A female peregrine**

Sachin was – *Sachin*. What a character! What a hawk! A good-sized hawk with a good conformation, fast and powerful, a dextrous footer, and deadly in the stoop. It's hardly surprising, coming from the much-sought-after strain bred by Nick Wilkinson.

She was entered at rooks and from her earliest days in the field showed signs of being the exception rather than the rule. After two seasons flying at rooks and crows I got the opportunity of returning to the grouse moors of Scotland for the first time in a dozen years, the only problem being I didn't have a game-hawk or a youngster to train on as such. So, I headed North with *Sachin*, and it didn't take her long to adapt to this new style of flight and new quarry – a measure of her intelligence. Things could easily have gone wrong in the first week when she was put up over several false points (Not from my dog, I might add). After one of these false points there were some surprised and admiring looks from the field as she closed her wings and dropped straight down to the fist from her pitch. I find it a big advantage to have longwings made to the fist as there are often times when there is nowhere practical to throw a lure out, such as on sodden plough, soft snow, or tall cover. Conversely, I have never made a shortwing to the lure during training although I do carry a dead lure in the field for emergencies. Once we returned to the lowlands it was back to flying corvids out of the hood.

The following year she was started off at grouse again and flew even better, having already learned the game, so well that on returning South I decided not to fly her at rooks and crows again, because of the added risk of loss or accident, and to keep her for game-hawking. After she had had the rest of the season off, we lost access to the moor. It was back to the normal day-job for her.

Flying a dual-purpose hawk meant that everything did not always run smoothly. Twice in Scotland, when efforts to serve her had failed, she refused the lure and sailed off the moor and was tracked down in the valleys on crows.

In the lowlands it had taken me several years to win over the rather prickly farmers and shooters. Eventually they begrudgingly accepted that I was only after corvids and was no threat to their gamebirds, although I rarely ever met any of my detractors when I had a crow in my hand to embellish my argument. On a miserable day of dark clouds and drizzle I had slipped *Sachin* at a small group of rooks a fair way off. I thought they were far enough away from a small conifer plantation to afford her a good chance, but that didn't turn out to be the case. *Sachin* was heading back to the lure at 200 feet when she suddenly dropped out of the sky and failed to reappear. I made my way over to find her breaking into a cock pheasant she had killed. I sorted her out, hooded her, and stuffed the pheasant into my pocket. The field was harrowed and flat and the pile of feathers stuck out like a sore thumb; so I began picking them up, carrying them to a nearby rabbit warren, and stuffing them down a hole. When I had finished and was about to set off for home I was startled to see a Landrover parked in the field from where two of the local shooters had been watching my nefarious activities. Bang to rights I think is the expression!

Sachin was not a text-book hawk and had her idiosyncrasies, but her flying style and character more than made up for that. She could be headstrong and wayward; indeed there seemed to be times when she spent more nights out than I did. In Yorkshire, following a flight at rooks, I tracked her down only to find nothing but her transmitter and a few black feathers. Needless to say I was out from dawn to dusk each day. She hadn't strayed much outside a radius of five miles or so but I seemed always to be just one step behind. One afternoon I was at a farmhouse where the farmer told me she had been perching on his garden fence that morning. One morning I was lure-swinging in a field where a farm-worker was ploughing. When I went over to explain the situation to him, he told me how she had been feeding on a crow the previous afternoon and he had thought it odd that she didn't move away from the tractor and he had had to drive round her. He even showed me the scene of the kill, adorned black feathers. When I explained to him that if he had dropped his coat over her, then rang the number on the flying jesses, he could have made himself £100, he looked as upset as I was. Another day she had come down near a shooting-party on a hare that had just been shot, but then thought better of it, and departed. She was out for five days before she came in to the lure – five ounces over flying-weight, I might add.

Worse was to come several years later down in Berkshire. The spring clip on the transmitter snapped and, unlike her time out in Yorkshire, there was not a single sighting. A bird-watcher did call me one day after he had spotted her on a pylon, but it turned out to be a wild hawk. This time she was out for thirteen days before coming in to the lure at the same place I had originally slipped her. This time she was six ounces above her flying weight and scarred around her eyes and nares from battling with corvids but otherwise in good condition.

She had developed her own style of crow-hawking (not traditional rook-hawking, granted) that was influenced, no doubt, by her excursions on the moor. She would slip off downwind, lulling the corvids into a false sense of security before heading back upwind and gaining height. Once well positioned she would deliver her devastating stoop at the now panicking flock, and rarely missed. It was not, as I said, text-book falconry but nonetheless most enjoyable to watch.

One of her more unusual feats is worth recording, taking place on a glorious day in September 2006.

Shortwings, particularly sparrowhawks, have been known to make a meal of garden birds foolish enough to stray too close to their bow-perch. Longwings usually have a more pacifist attitude to garden

59

birds, even eyeing them with head upturned, to all intent as if looking at them affectionately. Not so *Sachin*. A family of recently-hatched blackbirds were habituated to life in the garden. *Sachin*, only a few days out of the aviary, post-moult, and still fat after the summer's excesses, was weathering on the lawn. The adult female took exception to the presence of the hawk. Mick and I were watching her mobbing *Sachin*. When she flew over *Sachin*'s head the hawk launched herself off the block in an attempt to snatch the bird out of the air. We laughed. "That blackie had better watch herself," I said, "or she will end up as hawk-food," before we retired down to The Bay Horse for Sunday 'lunch'. On our return *Sachin* sat contentedly, foot-up, with a neat ring of blackbird feathers round her block.

Diary Extracts

Slipped at a mixed flock of corvids on a glorious September evening, she flew in her usual manner, slanting off downwind and then heading back and gaining height upwind. The corvids were spooked and made it to a line of trees while a pair of herons were accidentally flushed from a small pool. *Sachin* had continued in my direction and was then up at 400 feet, while the herons were at about 100 feet. When directly above them, against a clear azure blue sky, *Sachin* turned over, put in a vertical stoop, and bound to one of them. This was witnessed by a couple of astonished workmen who came over to ask if she always did that. "Oh yes," I replied, "but not usually on herons" (although it wasn't the first one she had killed).

January, 2008

Chesterfield. Out with MH.

Although it was five seasons since *Sachin* had flown at grouse, when I spotted a pair of mallard feeding in what looked like a perfect position for a set-up, I couldn't resist giving it a try. When training her to wait-on in Scotland, I used to wave my glove above my head and use a specific call. Even if she should remember these things, I still had my misgivings: this was lowland England and not a Scottish grouse moor; there would surely be no shortage of check in the vicinity in the form of the local corvid population and she wouldn't be able to resist. I cast her off, giving the call and the signal. *Sachin* began to mount. When she was at her pitch of 400 feet, and perfectly positioned, I sent Mick in to flush. *Sachin* stooped vertically but struck the drake only a glancing blow, as it managed to make a small pool of water. *Sachin* sat nearby. Whilst I was thinking whether to fly again, *Sachin* took off with no prompting from me, and regained her pitch. Mick flushed the drake again. A perfect vertical stoop followed and this time she hit it hard, bowling it over and swinging round to claim her prize. *Sachin* died at the beginning of her tenth season. She flew to me, without being called, sat on a nearby post, and keeled over of a heart attack.

Cally: a female peregrine x saker hybrid

Cally was my first hybrid falcon. I have seen some striking peregrine x saker hybrids, large and dark, looking more like peregrines than sakers in their plumage. *Cally* did not fall into that category. If you were to walk past her on her block you wouldn't give her a second glance – nothing special aesthetically and not particularly large, flying at 1 lb 15½ oz – but boy, could she fly!

On her third day flying loose I was letting her find her wings in the field at the back of the house when she disappeared from view behind the treeline and failed to respond to the whistle. Unprintable remarks! I was annoyed with myself for leaving her up too long and allowing her to stray or land or both. I tracked her down to the field the other side of the tree-line where she was feeding up on an unfortunate barn owl she had killed.

She was one of those star hawks that turn up far too infrequently. From those earliest days on the wing she just wanted to fly, and any bird she saw she would chase relentlessly. It was merely a case of pointing her in the right direction. She took her first (common) gull in Scotland and never looked back. On our returning South she was flown at gulls (mostly common) over the Yorkshire Wolds and the sport was second to none. I never saw her beaten except when the gull made it to water. Her flights at common gulls (far from an easy quarry) rank amongst the finest sport I've ever witnessed.

This hawk was making a name for herself and was destined for stardom until she was electrocuted, as already described. It was an extremely sad loss.

To describe a flight at common gulls with *Cally*, I could choose pretty much any flight from any day in the diary.

Diary Extracts

September 28

A fine bright afternoon. Out over the Wolds with Dave Taylor, he hoping to enter his peregrine x saker.

Just outside Finber we spotted a flock of thirty or so common gulls, a good way off on the other side of the valley. A long slip, but after considering the pros and cons, I decided to fly *Cally*. The hawk had probably covered half the distance before the gulls saw her and lifted. It took her a while to fetch them but eventually she got on to a gull and put in a stoop that the gull jinked to avoid before starting to ring with the hawk doing likewise. The process was repeated when the gull evaded another stoop. On and on the flight went, in similar fashion, up to 400 feet. Eventually the gull began to tire and was driven down lower and lower after each stoop until the flight dropped below the horizon and out of sight. When we arrived we found her pluming her well-earned gull.

September 30

Outside Shiptonthorpe. Overcast.

Slipped *Cally* at a mixed flock of gulls loafing on the plough. They were quickly up and away, apart from a solitary adult great black-back that stood its ground defiantly. More unprintable remarks followed. My own fault for not taking more care in studying the flock before deciding whether to fly. If I had seen the greater black back I wouldn't have. *Larus marinus* almost left it too late before getting up, leaving the hawk on the plough with a foot full of feathers. The gull which moments before, the master of all he surveyed, had been exuding calm authority, was now seriously stressed and flying as though his life depended on it. *Cally* got herself airborne and took up the chase. Once the gull had got above 200 feet it began to ring, and the hawk did likewise. A classic *haut vol* ensued; higher and higher the two birds rose battling for aerial supremacy.

As the flight ascended it also drifted downwind. I wouldn't like to hazard a guess as to the height they reached. I'm quite confident in putting forward any figure up to 400 feet. Judging on the basis of a pylon being 200 feet and imagining double that is not too difficult, but anything above that and my assessment becomes a little vague. How some falconers say with confidence that their hawk waits on at 1,000 feet I do not know, but back to the flight in hand. Now I was struggling to keep the two birds in view – no bin's with me as per usual. Finally, I couldn't see the hawk anymore and could only just make out the gull. I thought she must have set her wings, and produced the lure. At the same moment as I started to swing, I saw the gull begin to fall to earth. *Cally* had bound to it! I had a fair bit of ground to cover but it's amazing how much speed and stamina one can muster when time is of the essence. I arrived exhausted, panting hard, in the area where I thought hawk and quarry had come down. No sign. In my haste I had left the receiver in the van so I searched frantically around amongst the thigh-high set-aside. Twenty minutes or more had elapsed before I spotted my hawk. She was perched on a round bale on the other side of the road, some 200 yards away. She was streaked with blood (not hers) from the battle with the gull before it had managed to break free. I gave her a full crop for her splendid effort.

Incidentally, reading through the old literature, it's uncanny – but no coincidence – to note how many classic ringing flights begin with the hawk almost catching its quarry low down.

KP: a female peregrine x saker hybrid

KP had something of a chequered start to her life as a gull hawk. I was working as a delivery-van driver when I bought her but I figured I had the time to get a gull-hawk going and enjoy ten weeks or so of sport before it was curtailed through lack of daylight.

A large and powerful hawk, from her first days on the wing *KP* was buoyant and stylish – she certainly looked the part. Unfortunately, that's where her prospects of becoming a gull-hawk ended, at least for the time being. Try as I might I couldn't get her to take the slightest interest in gulls. My short season was in danger of passing me by and so, in view of her natural style of flight and having a good GSP, *Fudge*, I decided to turn to game. We spent six weeks or so game hawking, flying at pheasants and partridges. As the beet was thick and the fields relatively small and bounded by abundant cover, we didn't catch a great number but had some passable sport. By mid-October the shorter days had curtailed our flying and *KP* was left, for the time being at least on her block. I couldn't see any long-term future for the pair of us and so I contemplated selling her.

I ended up lending her to my friend Andy, a bird-controller, who needed another hawk for work. He had her for a couple of months but struggled to get on with her. At one point, when he was exasperated by a sick gull that was floating round his site, drawing in other gulls, *KP* wouldn't even look at it. Next, I loaned her to Chris, another bird-controller friend who had recently lost a hawk and was in need of a replacement.

On my return from India in March of the following year I took up a bird control job myself so picked up *KP* again from Chris. During her two loan spells she had still not shown any interest in gulls but had shown interest in corvids, although she hadn't actually caught any. After a while she began taking them and I started to train her for bird control as opposed to falconry. I flew her up to mid-summer and shortly before she was put down to complete her moult she took her first gull. After the moult I continued to use her for bird control and the number of gulls she caught steadily increased so that at some stage, I can't remember when, I made the decision to stop using her for bird control and re-kindle my original ambition to use *KP* as a gull-hawk. After being allowed free rein, and despite taking gulls with confidence, her predilection for crows remained. This meant that I should have to choose my slips very carefully indeed. It took a long time and much effort and hard work to get her wedded to gulls and completely 'off' corvids. It certainly didn't happen overnight and, indeed, it was the best part of three years before she was completely trustworthy. By this I mean that I could slip her at gulls, regardless of whether there were crows mingling with them or feeding in the vicinity, and be confident that she would not check. Even then we still had a few 'black days' in each season, but mostly in situations in which little blame could be attached to the hawk. Some of these occurred when she was making her way back to me after having either put the quarry in or been beaten by it, and perhaps a lazy or senile old crow would come flapping along right underneath her. On one such occasion her stoop split a rook right open, disembowelling it in the process. On another occasion, *KP* had knocked a herring gull down into a lake, breaking its wing, and was waiting on as I made my way down with the dog to retrieve it for her. I had noticed a half-albino crow passing but had thought little of it. As the dog was on her way back with the gull, I looked up – no hawk overhead. Just then I heard the commotion of a flock of angry corvids. Sure enough, *KP* had killed the half-white crow.

Although these odd 'black days' were not altogether her fault, especially considering her start in life, she still knows there is no reward for her in killing the black birds. On a gull she is totally relaxed, allowing me to help her out in any way with her quarry, but on a crow she hunches over at my approach, expressing her displeasure. It took a while but she did begrudgingly come to accept having a crow removed from her without a tantrum and being hooded. Ten seasons under her belt, eight of them at gulls, and with almost 500 gulls to her credit, are testimony enough to the turn-around.

Like all hawks she has her idiosyncrasies. After being moulted in the aviary it is usually the best part of three weeks before I can pick her up from the block without a bate. She is misogynistic and dislikes children even more than women, which is not particularly uncommon (and hawks trained by women often dislike men). My daughter Emily is respectful of hawks and knows how to behave around them. *KP* has seen her all her life but the old hawk has never got over her mistrust. Emily has only to set foot in the garden for *KP* to behave like a deranged accipiter.

An experienced gull-hawk will not bind to a large gull over deep water but most will tolerate shallow splashes like those found on a water-logged field. Not so *KP*. If she comes down in the merest puddle she will instantly let go.

When gulls reach an area of water which is not too large, she waits on, knowing there is still a chance. This is something she would not do over a large lake. She panics the gulls with repeated feigned stoops that send them swirling about over the water. She has learned that sooner or later a gull will make the mistake of flying just a few feet wide of the water and giving her the chance she has been waiting for. The gull's mistake is usually its last. Obviously on these occasions the flight has descended into a mere rat-hunt, but I enjoy watching her do this, even if it not classic high-end sport.

Diary Extracts

March 17

Chesterfield. Blustery dry day.

Found a mixed flock of 100 gulls on waste ground west of the industrial estate. Not an ideal position: the busy M1 was far too close for comfort but downwind and between the gulls and me. The only sanctuary for the gulls would be water on the landfill site or the lake at Poolsbrook, both of them over a mile away to the south-west and west respectively. Gave *KP* a longish slip to get the gulls heading in the right direction. She initially went side-on with the wind before turning and beginning to gain height, soaring into the sky, and eating up the distance between the gulls and herself. As she closed in on the flock at 150 feet she shot up on her tail and then put in a stoop at an adult herring gull. She connected with a wing and the two birds came spinning down before the gull broke free close to the ground. The gull then had the advantage of a good lead as it rang up and headed downwind. From her lowly position *KP* flew upwind and used the contours of a bank to rise rapidly in her attempt to gain parity with the gull. She achieved it at 300 feet, with both of them over the motorway when *KP* was all over the gull and putting in shallow stoops and cuts without managing to get a foot to him. The flight had nearly drifted out of sight when both birds merged and began to fall earthwards. All I could see beneath them was houses. They came down in a small estate where I came across *KP* administering the *coup de grace* in a residential back garden. Nobody at home. I fed her up and departed, satisfied with a fine flight.

December 18

Carcroft. Cold with snow.

Small flock of mostly black-headed gulls plus a few herring gulls loafing 300 yards out across the fields. Slipped *KP* and she, after fetching them, surprisingly singled out a black-headed and a fine flight ensued. She put in stoop after stoop, all evaded, seemingly effortlessly, by the aerial skills of a most adroit gull. The flight continued, drifting dangerously close to a road where there were two office buildings close to where the birds eventually disappeared. I jumped into the van and raced round, arriving to find *KP* on the pavement pluming her prize. Afterwards I gave the gull the once-over and found it was plump and in good condition.

November 1

Rufforth. Torrential rain eventually eased but wind very strong.

Slipped *KP* at 50 gulls a good way out on the airfield. *KP* cut low into the wind, looking as though she was not making much headway on them, but fetched them eventually, shooting up on her tail to put herself among them. She put in a hard stoop at a herring gull which avoided it. A high throw-up, and the flight continued with both birds heading out of sight as the flight had turned downwind towards the landfill. I feared she might check at an easier gull or, worse still, at a crow. However, she stuck to her chosen quarry and was tracked down on it two miles away near the A59. A very fine effort in a near gale-force wind. *TB* and *Black Dwarf* each killed a crow.

Triple Trouble: a female peregrine x gyr x saker

Triple or *TT* was trained and flown at gulls by Dave Taylor over the border in Dumfries and Galloway. Dave enjoyed some good sport although not without its problems. She was not the tamest of hawks and could be wild, temperamental and wayward. On one occasion Dave had tracked her down to a small island. By the time he realised that she had moved on, the tide had come in - leaving Dave stranded on the island for the night. Highly amusing of course – when it happens to someone else. *Schadenfreude* is rife amongst falconers! Halfway through her second season Dave decided to concentrate all his time and effort on his jerkin and so he offered *Triple* to me. Unfortunately, as I was heading out to Australia, I couldn't take him up on his offer. On my return I was surprised to hear that Dave still had *Triple* after being let down by a couple of time-wasters. Arrangements were made and *Triple Trouble* was added to the mews. I flew her for the rest of the season and she didn't disappoint.

After the moult she moved up a gear, although at times I was flying her too high and letting her get above herself. I was creating my own problems but a day-off or two and washed meat or rabbit would bring

her back into line. Regardless of that, she was always a bit of a 'wild child', never more so than when she came down with a gull into a wood or copse. For some reason this caused her to resent my presence and sent her into a fit of bad temper, making her virtually unmanageable. She would refuse to be assisted in dealing with her kill, became very aggressive, and would bate furiously when picked up, even with her crop full. Dave had experienced similar behaviour. Her manners were totally different when on a gull out in the open. Due to her wild nature it was always a race against time if she killed out of sight or a long way off. Without my presence she would eat twice as fast and with two-thirds of a crop she would be difficult to pick up.

One day in Lancashire I arrived too late when she had already departed. I eventually caught up with her well after dark, roosting in a tree. In the moonlight I tried to entice her with the dead lure, but to no avail. She came down at first light, still with a good crop on her.

The last I saw of *Triple* was a week before the end of her third season. She had flown gulls on passage over the brow of a hill, a carbon copy of flight she had made three days previously when I had picked her up on her gull on public land not far from a small town. The signal was good and constant – she was down. I jumped in the van and drove round. And then there was nothing – no signal and no sign. Powermax Marshall transmitters just don't behave like that. Even if she had been spooked and moved on, I should still have got a signal. I drove around for miles, with the roof-aerial on, I had the kite up for a week or more, and I went through all the usual processes when a hawk is lost, but deep down I knew I was wasting my time.

A year later, in the same location, I was exercising *KP* late in the day. When I cast her off and allowed her to gain height, and she had circled round a few times, I reached in my pocket for the lure to begin her work-out. At that moment she stooped into a distant field and did not re-appear. "That's odd," I thought. "There can't be any gulls down there." When I reached the field there was no sign. There was a good signal. She must have been close but I didn't seem to be getting any closer although I had gone through a small copse, crossed another field, and arrived at a thick hedge, on the other side of which was a housing-estate. There were no more signals. Darkness fell within the hour and, searching for the signal, I had a sense of *déjà vu*.

The following morning, still with no signal, I walked round swinging the lure – going through the motions – and soon decided to retrace my steps from where I had last seen her and where I had received the last signal. The land was still white from the three or four inches of snow that had fallen the previous day. When I reached the spot where I had seen her stoop and started heading in the direction I had then taken, I discovered that there were two sets of footprints in the snow! I followed them to outside the housing estate where the signal had failed. After finding a snickle-way through to the houses I walked round the estate, testing for a signal, with net curtains twitching and televisions no doubt being hastily stuffed into lofts and garden sheds. Before long I was approached by a man who asked me if I had lost a falcon which, he said to my relief, he had in his garden. He led me to his house and there on his back lawn sat *KP*, a shining light amongst his motley collection of owls, a kestrel, the obligatory Mexican parrot, and the only two hawks of any note, an immature male goshawk that he said he was getting rid of because he could do nothing with it, and a gyr x saker that he flew occasionally but it didn't catch anything! I quizzed him but not too intently. After all, he didn't have to approach me. He could have kept *KP* or sold her on and I would have been none the wiser. He insisted he had thought the hawk was lost – but why had he not waited around to see if there was a falconer in attendance? Why had he taken the battery out of the transmitter as soon as he got home rather than hanging it up on his front door? I had to mention *Triple* going missing a year before. He *said* he knew nothing about that. Perhaps it's me. Maybe I'm just paranoid!

On the subject of telemetry, another slight digression I grant you, but as a falconer it has always been the bane of my life!

Other falconers seem to splash out on receiver and transmitters and that's that, job done. But over the years I have had never ending problems ("why always me" in the words of Mr Balotelli), although admittedly some of them have been self inflicted. It seems to be a constant tail of woe, receivers not working properly, or the transmitters themselves, with a new battery packing up after one day, etc.

Hawks returning with the aerial missing or a broken spring and the whole transmitter missing or, worse still, deck or deck feathers missing along with the transmitter. I have even had a hawk return wearing what's left of the transmitter having been smashed in half! God Knows!

There is nothing more annoying than losing a transmitter out of one's pocket, or the back of the van (not switched on of course), an expensive mistake. Falling flat on your back on hard ground doesn't seem to do the receiver a lot of good! It was even worse for Nigel up in Scotland when he had inadvertently left his receiver on the ground and his then girlfriend (not sure whether this was the reason for the split) reversed over it in the four wheel drive.

I once managed to leave my receiver in a field overnight, not realising I had left it until the following afternoon, when it was time to fly the hawk. I drove the 20 odd miles with a feeling of trepidation, chuntering to myself about what an idiot I am. I was mightily relieved to find it exactly where I had left it.

Over the years I must have spent a small fortune on telemetry.

One slight caveat when a hawk is picked up on a kill or returns to the lure minus her transmitter, I find it very relaxing (when compared with the anxiety of tracking the hawk herself) and a test of one's tracking skills to hunt down the little blighter. I have retrieved a transmitter from a frozen pond with the use of a long branch, whittled down, magnet strapped to the end. Improvise, adapt and overcome as Army Mick would say. I was not quite so lucky when *KP* had hit her gull several times over a pond, and knocked the transmitter off thus sending it to a watery grave.

Son of Hellboy: a jerkin (male gyrfalcon)

For many years a gyr was not a hawk I had any aspirations to fly. The peregrine was always the hawk of choice, an opinion reinforced in falconry down the ages. Stevens was an advocate of gyrs, and much as I enjoy his works dedicated to the species, they still didn't fire my enthusiasm to rush out and get my hands on one. In relatively recent times gyrs have become more readily available, but no less expensive. Even if I had wanted one, they were well beyond the reach of this impecunious falconer. Dave had flown a few and was always singing their praises. Every time I spoke to him he was forever telling me that I had to fly one, so when I had a change of circumstances and the money was burning a hole in my pocket, a gyr it was to be. I wanted a falcon but couldn't acquire one as all the gyrs bred in the U.K. seemed to be heading out to the Middle East, so a jerkin it had to be.

The first time I set eyes on *Son of Hellboy* I was impressed. What a striking-looking hawk! I had high hopes for this dark beauty. Incidentally, among the polymorphic extremes in the species my

preference has always been for the dark morph, *obsoletus*, over most falconers' favourite, the white morph, *candicans*. A white gyr, or cast of them, taking a red kite, as famously depicted by Joseph Wolf in 1856, certainly looks spectacular, but to me at least, so does the sight of a black gyr taking a predominantly white quarry such as a gull. Anyway, I'm drifting off into aesthetics rather than practicalities. To be honest, it doesn't matter if the hawk is pink with blue spots as long as it flies like the wind. On the other hand I have no time for pretty lawn ornaments.

Hellboy's training and entering all went remarkably smoothly and he had an impressive first season. The only slight blemish in his character was that in the first few months he had a propensity to bate prior to flying while he was still in the hood. Fortunately he grew out of this trait, aided by a little subterfuge on my part.

The literature states that in the wild gyrs hunt in a different style from peregrines, one that more closely resembles the hunting strategy of a merlin. Indeed his speed, style, manoeuvrability, ease of mounting, and high throw-ups did resemble the action of a giant merlin. *Hellboy*'s preferred method of attack is to strike rather than bind to his gull, a tactic that I'm surprised more hawks don't adopt. It seems to be more efficient than binding to such a large quarry, having to control it in the air as well as in the descent to the ground. More often than not *Hellboy* stoops at a wing, sending the gull spinning to earth if he connects, but he will also stoop at the head of the quarry, resulting in it falling and dropping to earth as if shot. It always looks more spectacular at a greater height or a longer distance when it appears he has barely touched it. In every way he has been everything that I have heard and read about gyrs – and more. When he killed his third gull his weight had risen to 2 lb 9 oz. His behaviour and mannerisms had not altered, nor, so I thought, his flying. It took me the best part of a fortnight to realise he was just going through the motions, flying cunning, doing all the right things, but with no intention of actually getting his feet on a gull. A little sharpening up in condition soon had him back on track.

Diary Extracts

November 6

Sunny spells out at Rufforth.

Looked for a slip for *Hellboy* but no gulls on the airfield and in the fields – only large flocks that didn't look to be an ideal slip. Deliberated on the best course of action before putting up the most suitable flock to give them a start. It took *Hellboy* a while to fetch them but he didn't disappoint. After he had singled out an adult herring gull it was all hard stoops followed by vertical throw-ups, a joy to watch. The gull was hard-pressed and turned downwind and towards me. As they came overhead I could see *Hellboy*'s tactics. The hard stoops he was putting in were aimed at the gull's wing rather than the body. I think it is a good strategy, although it does make it easier for the gull to shift away. After several misses he went for Plan B. When the gull avoided yet another stoop he threw up and bound to it from underneath. He had a poor hold though, and when they came down to earth the gull broke free – but its reprieve was only temporary.

February 19

Fine, spring-like day, light breeze. York.

Spotted a flock of gulls off the A59 near the Red Lion but as soon as I pulled up they were away. Although nowhere as intelligent as the crow family, the local gulls have definitely realised that my van means trouble! As I drove back round the lanes the gulls were beginning to settle again – at least some of them were – and I parked up out of sight in the Red Lion car park. As I got *Hellboy* ready the gulls were circling at 100 feet some 200 yards away. He was fidgety, eager to fly and when I struck the braces and unhooded him he was away immediately. This is not always the case with him, as more often than not he likes to rouse and weigh up the situation before launching into battle. The gulls made off, ascending towards Poppleton with *Hellboy* mounting at 60° in pursuit. He fetched them at the edge of visibility and put in a rattling good stoop ending in a noticeable contact and the gull began to fall to earth at the edge of the village. I jumped in the van and drove to where I thought *Hellboy* would be, but no sign. Tracked him down to a field a few hundred yards away beyond a group of houses, where angry corvids were giving his whereabouts away. The large herring gull he was on just about breathing its last. It must have recovered from the initial stoop on or close to the ground, but not enough to get much further and save its life. A decent effort.

January 2

Another fine afternoon. Cornwall.

Spotted gulls off the Grampound Road. Unfortunately, by the time I'd parked the van up I'd lost my bearings somewhat and entered the wrong field. The 200 or so herring gulls had taken wing 150 yards behind me and downwind, but the braces had been struck and *Hellboy* was away. The gull he'd singled out was a good one. The hawk was working hard, throwing up high on its tail after each stoop but not getting a foot to it. The battle continued with both birds ringing up for aerial supremacy. A fine flight, pushing 600 feet, with *Hellboy* still cutting at the gull before they were lost to view, drifting downwind. I had to track *Hellboy* down to the outskirts of St Stephen and was disappointed to find that he had failed to kill after such a good effort.

Marsh on point

CHAPTER FIVE

Days from the Diary

I will attempt to keep this fairly short, as describing flight after flight can become repetitive, and with this in mind I shall try to mix good flights up with less remarkable days to show the true nature of the sport. In truth I have forgotten more good flights than I can remember, as it is only in relatively recent years that I have started to keep a diary.

March 29

A clear day. Yorkshire.

Skye is being bothered by red kites. Yesterday she just flew round, alarm-calling, and was reluctant to come in to the lure. Today she was slipped at 20 gulls but a kite appeared and she went for it, with the kite jinking to avoid her, until the two birds started to ring and they ascended with impressive speed. My hawk, being the faster climbing of the two, got above the kite and was able to put in a stoop. Kite rolled on its back to meet the hawk with its feet. I don't think *Skye* was serious about binding to the kite but it made a good spectacle. They rang up again to a great height but when *Skye* got in perfect position she did not stoop again. The flight gave a little insight into the sport enjoyed by our ancestors.

October 5

Rufford.

Slipped *KP* at gulls out on the plough. She went up well, singling out a great black-back but as the flight was developing nicely the gull threw up the contents of its crop and *KP* floated down on it and was left standing on the plough looking rather foolish. The same thing happened last week down in Berkshire

October 22

At Rufford on a bright and breezy morning with M.H.

Slipped *KP* at a good-sized flock and initially lost sight of her until we saw her flying back towards us and chasing a black-headed gull that was making for a small stretch of water. We ran down to keep it on the wing and *KP* kept working hard to get above the gull and putting in stoop after stoop, which were all evaded by the gull. We could see the hawk had her beak open, but she kept at her gull, showing the greatest perseverance until she eventually caught it – out of sight, unfortunately.

September 10

Fine and sunny, out with Mick and Wendy. (Beware of Hoodies).

Slipped *Sicknote* off the A9 outside Invergordon at a small flock of rooks out on the stubble. The flight went over the hill and out of sight, but the angry corvids signalled a kill, so no time to waste getting to the scene. Couldn't believe it when I arrived to find the tiercel rolling around with a whacking great hooded crow, fortunately without injury or feather damage.

Tried *KP* at gulls around Invergordon Industrial Estate, but I could tell as soon as she left the fist that she was not that interested. She put in a half-hearted effort before raking off and we eventually tracked her down on… a hooded crow! Never caught one before and now two in the same day! What a pain in the arse *KP* can be at the start of the season.

Poor Wendy, owner of the Balconnie Hotel at Evanton. She was very interested in the hawks, hence being invited out. It was left to Mick to explain to her why I was not a happy man after *KP*'s exploits.

September 11

Scotland – Thurso.

Took the hawks on a trip up to Thurso to check out the surf. Flat! Slipped *Sicknote* at a mixed flock. He singled out a jackdaw it turned into a rat-hunt when it dived under a sheep with *Sicknote* cutting back and forth. Jackdaw made a break for it and was taken. Flew *KP* at gulls near Invergordon. She didn't look interested and went for a crow before eventually drifting off downwind and taking a common gull following the plough. Another course of washed meat and rangle, methinks.

January 9

Corcroft, cold and murky.

Slipped *Skye* at a mixed flock loafing out over open fields. She singled out a common gull and flew it for all her worth right to the outskirts of the town. Up and down, stoop after stoop, but *Larus canus* was shifting so easily it looked as if she would never get a foot to it. She evidently thought the same and checked at a passing great black-back. It had a long lead, which *Skye* soon made up and clipped it a couple of times before binding to it but the gull broke free and the flight continued out of sight. The gull had reached water over the brow and *Skye* returned to the lure and was taken up. Got to Rufforth at dusk, just in time for a flight. *KP* fetched her gull and killed a herring first stoop.

February 2

Rufforth, rain and cold.

Slipped *KP* at a mixed flock and lost sight of her immediately. Ended up tracking her down over a mile away pluming the common gull she had taken. It must have been a decent flight but seeing none of it defeats the whole purpose of the sport.

January 21

Harewood Whin. Cold.

Slipped *PG* at the landfill site where she gained height before heading for the gulls. In the distance at the back of the site she hit her gull, which staggered and recovered. Then the flight was on, with both birds heading east. The gull gained height but was always hard-pressed, with *PG* all over it, following every twist and turn, as well as putting in several shallow stoops. On and on the flight continued ascending to 450 feet until I was watching two specks in aerial combat against a glorious sky, bloodshot with the early morning sun. Hawk and gull disappeared from sight. When *PG* didn't return I was praying she had caught it, after such a great flight from the youngster. Tracked her down on the ground next to a pond, no sign of the gull. Fed her up.

Triple Trouble got in four or five stoops at an adult herring before losing the initiative, with the gull looking to have made good its escape, but *TT* resumed and worked hard to get back on terms. Yet, after several more stoops, she eventually set her wings and came in to the lure.

Slipped *KP* at gulls circling at 100 feet and she went at her best pace, wings pumping hard to gain height. She switched briefly to a solitary adult herring coming back in my direction before changing her mind and heading back towards the main flock, that was now almost out of sight. Tracked her down on her gull 5 miles away!

Tried *Triple* again. She cut a herring down, breaking its wing, but it fell on to a frozen patch of water. She flew back and forth, cutting at it until it was almost dead, before she bound to it. Luckily for me, as the ice was only thin, she dragged it to the bank.

February 15

Bury.

KP took a nice gull. Interesting, because she bound to it over water – something she usually doesn't do. She controlled it well in her feet and managed to glide down away from the water, making dry land by a couple of feet. *TT* put a gull down into water after a good effort. After she killed a rook in a tree yesterday, it's a shame she didn't take it!

February 27

Fine ringing flight by *KP* at an adult herring that eventually beat her. Later on got a long slip on the back fields, *KP* flying hard and high again. It looked as if she was switching from gull to gull before they made the lake. Thought she was heading back to me but I hadn't noticed a passing great black-back which she bound to first stoop.

March 6

Sunday. A 'mini' gull-meet. Dave T. down here from Dumfries with his jerkin. Absent T. Pick. Thanks for keeping us waiting around for an hour!

Dave and I headed for the Triton Inn at Sledmere where Ray and Greg had stayed overnight. We all set off for Scarborough.

Located a small flock outside Seamer. Dave first up with his jerkin. The youngster put up a decent effort, almost getting a foot to it at one point, but was beaten and then called in. *Triple* next. I wasn't 100% content with the slip, so when *Triple* didn't go I was quite happy to hood her back up. Found another flock following the plough on the other side of Seamer. Not ground I knew, so Dave went over to ask the tractor driver if we could fly. He returned relating that "Giles" said O.K. so long as we gave him £5 for the Children's Hospice. We left it on principle but I liked Greg's idea: "Let's tell him we'll give him a tenner if we catch a gull and if we don't he gets fuck-all."

Failing to find another slip, we returned to the opposite end of the field and decided to fly. If the hawk killed on his land and we had to pick her up we would give him his "Lady Godiva" and if not then we had done nothing that required access. Slipped *Triple* and she set off low in an attempt to mug an unsuspecting gull, but they all rose and a decent flight at a herring ensued with *Triple* ringing it to 350 feet before setting her wings. As I produced the lure she put in a lovely stoop into the fields behind us at what turned out to be a wild peregrine.

Dave tried his jerkin again near the landfill at Seamer Carr. He went up well, putting gulls down into a pond before switching to a crow that he put into a bush.

Next up was *Triple* at gulls loafing on a recycling site's roof. She soon fetched them and flew an adult herring back towards us and bound to it, coming down with it a few yards from where we were parked.

KP had a long slip at gulls around the landfill, but as she gained height she drifted left towards gulls on the roofs of the industrial estate. Lots of stoops and throw-ups but she failed to kill.

Dave tried the jerkin on the landfill but he was confused by the number of swirling birds and ended up being mobbed by corvids.

Spotted a small flock of gulls outside Seamer. I went round by the B-road to slip *KP* into the wind, whilst Dave, Ray, and Greg positioned themselves on the other side of the gulls, hopeful of the flight going overhead – which it did, with *KP* flying a herring gull that she bound to first stoop about a hundred yards from them.

While looking for a last slip for the jerkin. Greg spotted a winged greylag. When he suggested we administer the *coup de grace*, off went Greg and me on our wild goose chase.

Dave drove round until dusk but failed to find a slip for the jerkin.

The day has been far from a first-rate showing, with Dave's jerkin still learning and my hawks too high, but things could have gone worse. On the bright side, as I write up the record I am looking forward to a roast goose dinner.

October 19

KP took a second-year herring gull at Holme-on-Spalding Moor. Nothing noteworthy about that other than that she killed it stone dead in the stoop – the first instance I've known of it happening while gull-hawking.

December 12

Lincolnshire.

Slipped *Hellboy* at blackheads. He flew off into the wind to gain height and at 450 feet came back at the gulls, which by that time were over water. Put in a rattling good stoop, threw up and switched to distant gulls before turning and heading back for the blackheads, at a greater height, to put in another tremendous stoop – but no throw-up. Made my way over towards where I could see him on his gull. At 150 yards away he flew back to me. Very puzzled, I walked over to the gull. Found it was a dead carrier bag. Baby hawks!

    KP, who flew like the wind yesterday, put in a half-hearted effort, sat on a bank and refused the lure. What a joy it is to be a falconer!

October 21

The tail-end of hurricane Gonzalo hit Blighty today, blowing a hoolie at Peckfield.

Slipped *KP* at a few gulls floating about in the wind. Lost sight of her for a while before seeing her again, working into the wind, high up over the wood. She locked onto an adult great black-back but after a bit of a ding-dong she wisely switched to an immature herring. Gulls being masters of strong wind she looked distinctly second favourite but her speed, power and agility proved decisive and she got a foot to him at 250 ft and brought him down.

    Hellboy had a coursing up and down flight at a great black-back, disappearing over the tree line and coming back into the lure several minutes later. Don't think he was 100% committed to getting a foot to him.

November 14

I had been flying *Hellboy* to the lure during the week whilst down in Hykeham, but on the spur of the moment I decided to let him have a dip at the local gulls. A crosswind slip in a stiff breeze, soon losing sight of him as the gulls were up and away. Spotted him in the distance flying full on at the flock of thirty or so gulls, up at 300 ft. He gained rapidly, split a gull from the flock and put in a hard stoop, missed then flew up on his tail putting him in pole position. Another rattling good stoop followed, which the gull avoided. At this point I was getting slightly concerned. The flight was now a long way off, I didn't know what sort of terrain he was over or how on earth to get there if he caught the gull. So produced the lure and was pleased and relieved to get an instant response. I'm getting to like this hawk!

December 5

Gulls circling at 200 ft over Pilsworth.

Slipped *KP* from a good distance and rather than heading straight at the gulls she concentrated on gaining height. Not in rings, as a peregrine would, but, using the updraft from the bank she powered straight upwards at a 60 degree angle. The gulls had exited stage left as she continued to climb. Levelling out at 600 ft she was now pumping hard into the distance while my eyes strained to keep her in view. She then began to stoop but I couldn't see her intended quarry. A rattling vertical descent then, at 400 ft, *bang* – she hit her gull, binding to it and down they came. Jumped in the van, under the motorway and parked up by the supermarket. I had a fair idea where the hawk and quarry had come down and was taking note of the circling gulls. I was rather pleased with myself to come across her on her lesser black-back (magpies pinpointing her precise location) without taking the receiver from its case. A fine flight.

Time Bomb (tiercel) unlucky on the hill, *Marsh* flushing the grouse prematurely whilst the young hawk was out of position, resulting in a futile tail chase. *Skye* killed an adult herring.

February 9

KP not flown or fed yesterday but still a little high from her gorge on Saturday. Slipped at Pilsworth and she took her usual route, round the bank face then up and away, gaining height. She started stooping at a gull over the water and I figured that would be that but she left it, climbed again to 250 ft and then really put the power on heading in the direction of the supermarket. She fetched her gull, a lesser, getting in a hard stoop which the gull evaded but *KP* was up on her tail and on him again. A real *Battle of Britain* taking place, twists, turns, stoops and throw ups, the only trouble being they were over the motorway. The gull doubled back, no doubt heading for the sanctuary of the water, but *KP* clipped it in a stoop and the panic-stricken gull changed direction and the flight continued. Again the gull tried to head back towards the pond but the hawk hit it again, forcing it down. It tried to turn back towards the motorway but *KP* bound to it and down they came – but it looked awfully close to the main road from where I was standing. Made my way over to find her pluming her quarry on a footpath 10 yards from the road. Another great flight.

November 15

Early morning surf at Cayton, hawks loaded in the van, hoping for a flight.

Spotted a small group of gulls a fair way off, outside Binnington, unhooded *KP* and she was away. It was a long fetch and she flew in a wide arc, gaining height to 300 ft. The gulls turned, heading down wind, the flight coming back in my direction. *KP* had a lot of ground to make up but was pumping hard. She fetched her gull (herring) still up at 300 ft but by this time only 50 yards in front of me. Steepling up on her tail she got a foot to him first stoop and brought him down, right in front of me , on a nice grassy field, a stone wall shielding it from the farm house. What a change it makes to have a relaxing stress-free flight where there is no tracking involved and you're not running along at full pelt, stricken with anxiety wondering where hawk and quarry have come down and if she's ok.

November 21

Slipped *KP* at a decent sized flock, a good way off and 200 ft up. She flew with great determination, putting the gulls down into water before I lost sight of her. She appeared again at 400 ft heading for gulls by the supermarket and industrial area! She didn't kill, coming back over me, cruising around, not coming down to the lure for ten minutes or so. A tad high, methinks!

Tried *KP* later in the day, a similar slip and she didn't disappoint. She fetched her gull and got in two hard stoops, taking her well down and out of position, before powering up again. She flew her gull out of sight towards the sand banks, circling crows signalling the kill (lesser).

November 28

Bury

Gulls circling at 100 ft in a stiff breeze. Slipped *KP* from 300 yards downwind. She flew hard, eventually getting on her gull in the distance, she got in one stoop before the gull made the lake. She came back over at 300 ft, but only one thing on her mind, she ignored the lure and headed toward the industrial area. I saw her stoop, circling gulls denoting the kill, but where had she come down? Jumped in the van, arriving to find her in a small patch of grass, behind a billboard, so not visible to the hurly burly of the supermarket with its numerous people and cars, and in a pizza restaurant car park which was all but deserted, only one man had noticed her and he came over to take some pictures.

December 7

Harewood

No gulls about so went to the local landfill site, flew *Skye* to disperse the gulls and hopefully give me something to fly at. Hour or so later found a small flock of gulls at the back of the Red Lion at Knapton. Put them up before slipping *KP* and, although the slip was downwind, I figured the gulls would turn and head upwind towards the landfill and the sanctuary of water, and that *KP* would fly round the back of them, then gain height into the wind. Best laid plans!! Lost sight of her almost immediately, there were obviously more gulls further downwind. She failed to return. I followed the signal in the van and was more than a little concerned when I ran out of countryside and reached built up Acomb. Followed the signal down a side road of Beckfield Lane and was mightily relieved to see *KP* on her gull (herring) in the middle of Car Infant School playing fields. Slightly awkward scaling the 8 ft fence, especially on the way back with hawk on fist! *KP* is flying so well, fit and determined, that slips within a few miles of York are becoming unfeasible.

Long slip for *Hellboy* who flew well before he checked at a woodpigeon.

January 28

Overcast, Upper Poppleton

Slipped *KP* at 20 gulls which immediately made for the distant fishing lake, *KP* in hot pursuit. She reached parity with the gulls at 300t then turned her gull into the wind, gaining height, before getting in a shallow stoop which the gull avoided. There followed a twisting, turning tail chase, like a merlin on a lark, *KP* was too good for him, binding to her quarry at 200 ft.

February 7

KP a little high at 2 lb 5 ¾ oz but spotted a small flock of gulls outside Easingwold on the way up to Nick's so thought I'd give it a go. Got *KP* ready but the gulls had disappeared!

Found another small group of gulls further up the A19. Parked up and slipped the hawk. Gulls were up and away, a long fetch for the hawk, up at 400 ft, could only just see her in the distance. Lost sight of her as she banked left then caught sight of her again as she put in a rattling vertical stoop before binding to her gull (herring) on the second stoop. A long way off and when I was about half way there I realized I had left my receiver in the van (before I slip a hawk I say to myself "lure, whistle, food, telemetry" and if I forget to say this I invariably end up leaving something behind!). Hard going over the heavy ground I was reluctant to go all the way back to the van so, no problem, I shouldn't need it, I saw where she came down. I arrived at what I thought was the spot but no sign! Just when I was thinking I'd have to trek back to the van, a couple of crows gave away her whereabouts, another 200 yards further on. It goes to show how distances are hard to judge.

March 5

Pilsworth again. *KP* up at 500 ft, into the wind towards Bury. Couldn't see if she was on a gull but started to get a little concerned as to where she would end up if she was, when she turned and headed back in my direction. There were gulls behind me up at 200 ft, rapidly departing towards Heywood, *KP* in hot pursuit. I could only just see her as she put in a tremendous stoop and didn't see a throw up but she came back into the lure several minutes later. Tried *KP* again later. The gulls were up and away and the hawk didn't immediately come into view. Then she appeared, quite low over the trees and pond before shooting up at 60 degrees and taking up the chase. Gulls up at 300 ft and well away, the hawk had a lot to do. She was soon bearing down on the gulls over the industrial estate. Her chosen gull turned, heading back from whence it came. Twisting and turning as the gull dropped down *KP* managed to clip it but instead of making the pond the gull turned again, trusting his wings. The hawk clipped it once more before binding to it over the trees.

October 28

Cornwall

Difficult to find gulls in a decent position for *KP*. Eventually settled on a small group of herrings near the Grampound/Fraddon crossroads. Went to put the transmitter on but the mount that Gav had made by soldering two empty bullet cases together had snapped off (unfortunately Gavin's skills as a falconer and a fisherman don't appear to stretch to welding!). I cable-tied the spring together then cable-tied that to the aylmeri.

I watched her up and down on what looked like a good gull until they were out of sight down the valley. She didn't return so it was out with the receiver. After some confusion I eventually tracked the transmitter down to a field in the region I had last seen her stooping the gull. The spring had snapped off. Searched until dark but no sign.

October 29

Dawn to dusk whistling and lure swinging but no sign, not that I expected to see her today if she'd killed the gull.

October 30

Mist and rain, not good! Searched all morning, no sign. Broke for lunch. Out again, weather clearing, tried the other side of Fraddon which I hadn't tried in the morning. Saw a bird of prey on top of a big chimney stack, probably just another buzzard, but swung the lure blew the whistle and in she came. Blood-stained from the gull she had killed on Monday, she was back at flying weight following her gorge two days ago.

September 5

0730 hours Nasri *198 g. Tiercel 600 g. Avonmouth on a hot humid day, fly-spraying the waste station.*

Found a nice grassy plateau so decided to give *KP* some exercise to the lure. However, *KP* had other ideas and after losing sight of her I spotted her high over the industrial estate roofs where thirty or so gulls had been loafing. She threw up over the fast departing gulls, missed with a stoop and then chased an adult herring gull back towards the buildings before binding to it and coming down on the large flat area of coarse gravel (fortunately not damaging her outer primaries which are still in the blood). A little premature, but her first kill of the season.

Horrendous afternoon on Britain's motorway network, what joy! Arriving tired and stressed at Moss Moor at 1915 hrs just in time for a quick fly.

Nasri, 188 g, turned tail on a good lark, then got the better of one after a couple of rings but it bailed and put in amongst sheep. Tried the reflush but the lark kept low and flew down to the road. Then saw *Nasri* having a ding-dong with a wild merlin but in the fading light could not tell which hawk was which and who was the aggressor. Maybe the wife or mother of the jack she caught the other day out for revenge! *Nasri* eventually returned beak open, panting so at least she had a good work out.

Young tiercel, 585 g. Tried feeding him on the fist in the camper but it was all that I could do to get him to stand up. Retired to the Ram's Head.

January 25-26

Sussex

Couldn't find any gulls all day, *KP* flown to the lure, decided to do likewise with *Triple* last thing. She did one circuit then disappeared down the valley where a few corvids were loitering. No response to the lure. Took out the receiver, a constant signal so made my way down. The signal was coming from a large area of swamp and reeds on the other side of the river, Fortunately there was a bridge but that turned out to be the only filip. I followed the signal through 7 ft high reeds into the swamp, at times sinking down to my waist, grabbing hold of reeds or branches to prevent myself sinking further and to haul myself out, all using one arm so as to keep the receiver dry. I abandoned the search as the light faded, not even being totally convinced that she was in there. After changing into some dry clothes I triangulated the signal which confirmed that she was in the swamp. Still in darkness I checked the signal again first thing before waiting for daylight then setting off into the swamp again. The further I went the more treacherous it became. It was like a water bed, at times sinking to my chest and having to spread my weight to prevent me from going under. Eventually I made it to the hawk who was at the bottom of the reeds and struggling to get out. After the initial shock of seeing me burst into view through the reeds, I managed to pick her up ok. Getting back out of there with hawk on fist was tough going. *Triple* had sustained a cut to her right wing (nothing serious) and broken four tail feathers! I couldn't determine what she had killed from her casting later in the day.

October 26 (Tracking Sunday)

Accrington on a blustery day with Rich and Chris.

Marked a jack snipe for *Gnome*, Chris's tiercel, but he raked off and had an *al fresco* bath (his favourite thing in life!) then disappeared downwind before Chris could pick him up. Rich and I waited an age and eventually Chris returned but without his hawk and so we returned to the vehicle to set off tracking. The tiercel was many miles away so we decided it would be safe enough for me to head in the other direction and get *Hellboy* flown.

Slipped *Hellboy* at a small group of common gulls off the Hasledon Road but lost sight of him almost immediately and he failed to return to the lure. The signal was good but I was on high ground so I was thinking I should probably go back for my van but against my better

Above & right: *KP*. End to successful flights

judgment I pressed on … and on … Ended up right down in the valley, scrambling down a ravine, over a river and up the other side. I could see a sports-field in the distance and I figured that's where he probably was, on his gull. Not so. Having reached built-up Accrington, no nearer to him, it confirmed what I was thinking all along, that he was still flying. A long, long haul back to the van. By the time I'd negotiated the ravine and the river (having a much needed drink from it) I had to stop for a breather. I was feeling pretty ropey as it was, after a heavy night previously in the Park (the Park Public House, I hadn't been sitting on a bench drinking cider from a brown paper bag). I carried on but I lost my bearings. I eventually came across a road but I didn't recognise it. After walking along it for a mile or more I decided to double back to a farm house I had passed to ask for directions – but nobody home – just typical! In the middle of nowhere with no phone, no hawk and no van – brilliant. In desperation I stood in the middle of the road and flagged down a passing van to ask for directions. All I knew was that somewhere in the area was a small garden centre where I was parked and fortunately the driver of the van knew where it was and pointed me in the right direction. He kindly said he would have taken me there if his van had not been full of equipment.

Anyway, eventually back to my van and made my way to Accrington where I was getting a good signal from the opposite side of the town, but then it faded away, followed by my phone ringing (which I had previously left in the van despite Rich continuously telling me to take it with me when hawking. He is right of course but I always think that the fewer things I carry with me that I am likely to lose the better). It was Rich; *"Hi Nick, how much reward is on offer for finding this jerkin?"* Unbelievable. Rich and Chris had eventually caught up with *Gnome* near Burnley and on their return to Accrington had received a phone call from Chris's dad saying that someone had reported a "lost peregrine" sitting on a farm roof. They had gone to investigate and had called *Hellboy* in to the lure!

Just enough time left in the day to head back to the hill and fly Richard's tiercel, *Polack*. Soon got a point with *Todd*, *Polack* waiting on nicely at 400 ft, up gets a pipit! We tried desperately to get another point but *Polack* had spotted distant pigeons and had raked off. Here we go again. Rich and Chris had a head-start as I had to feed up *KP* and my tiercel but we both came round a corner in our respective vehicles and met up on the same street in the middle of Oswaldtwistle where Rich then pinpointed *Polack* in a back yard eating his pigeon, just before dark. What a day. Time for me to present the lads with their 'reward' in the Park.

Triple Trouble out of the moult

CHAPTER SIX

'Moor' Days from the Diary

September 10

0730 hrs, Nasri *187 g, young tiercel 546 g.*

Fed the young tiercel a few mouthfuls in the garden of the Rose and Crown, getting steadier.

Nasri 184 g at 1000 hrs, early session at Tilshead. The first flight was a good one and a lovely ringing flight, up at 500 ft when *Nasri* was engaged by a wild kestrel/merlin (too far away to tell) and the flight was spoilt. Probably just as well, as they had drifted over the army firing range, red flags out! Next up another lark that looked good, but the hawk was all over it and at 150 ft it lost its bottle and was taken putting in. Another point and another good lark, a fine ringing flight ensued again, but *Nasri* was beaten by this lark and set her wings at 400+ ft. Almost caught a poor lark, but fortunately didn't, then turned tail on a good lark.

A while before the next point, a good lark and *Nasri*, flying with great determination, providing a fantastic ringing flight. On and on they went until the hawk started jinking, she had obviously fetched the lark, which was no longer visible and was trying to get a foot to him. The flight continued, the merlin only just visible against the clear blue sky. Finally she began to descend, but only in short stoops, then up again, as the lark was evading them and attempting to mount again. Eventually the lark, beaten, dropped for a clump of trees, although all I could see was the merlin stooping. Made my way over, but *Nasri* appeared floating around. What a shame she hadn't taken this one – a thrilling flight!

September 14

Quick hour at Accrington between work and the match (City v. Napoli). Blustery with showers. Brezhnev *186 g. Out with Rich and Chris.*

Two flights at good larks but the hawk set her wings on both occasions at no higher than 200 feet. Similar tale with Richard's hawk, twice at larks and once at a pipit. We decided that at the next lark we would let both hawks go and see what would unfold. Chris had marked a lark, which flushed. Richard slipped his hawk which initially didn't look over-interested until I slipped my hawk a couple of seconds later. *Brezhnev* powered up and Rich's hawk followed in earnest. A wonderful ringing flight followed with both hawks and lark striving for aerial supremacy. As the flight drifted downwind the three birds ascended to over 500 feet, where the lark disappeared from view. Commentary came from Chris (with the binoculars) before the hawks, too, went out of sight. We walked in their direction for five minutes and then began luring. After a while Rich's merlin came in to the lure. There was no sign of *Brezhnev*. We followed the faintest of signals until it was lost as we came down off the moor and picked up again on the farmland. The heading of the signal was a distant cottage, and, sure enough, when I arrived she was on the patio with the lark – a fitting end to a fantastic flight. Incidentally, this hawk was always frustratingly inconsistent. She could do it if she wanted to, but regardless of weight or conditioning, on too many days she just didn't. I thought maybe it was me, but Pete Smith had the same trouble with her in his attempts to fly snipe, as did Paul Dewing when he flew her at larks in the following season. Nick re-named the hawk *Duffy*. What's wrong with the names I give hawks?

September 3

Bodmin. Why Always Me 185 g at 1000 hrs. Light feed. Had her first bath! 181 g at 1600 hrs. Dry, bright sunny periods.

Half an hour or so before *Marsh* came on point. A decent lark and a nice ringing flight developing, the only problem being we were too close to the edge of the moor and at 300 feet the lark bailed for the pasture fields. *Why Always Me* must have been right on it for she jumped out of ditch with wet tail and covert feathers. Intended to leave her to dry out but *Marsh* was soon on point again and I decided to fly. Carbon copy of the first flight – the lark bailed for the gorse from 300 feet with the hawk stooping behind but failing to kill. Headed for the centre of the moor where *Marsh* came on point again. Another nice little ringer, but at the same height the lark dropped straight for me and was taken round my legs.

A short rest before continuing, then from another point the lark flushed prematurely and it was a good one. The lark climbed strongly, hawk likewise, and flying well to the left. As hard as the merlin was working she still didn't seem to make any headway on the lark but she never gave up. The lark suddenly stopped ringing and flew hard in a straight line in the direction of distant reeds with the hawk doing likewise but still below the lark. Once there it plummeted, the merlin likewise, but she failed to kill. Another rest, and then onwards and upwards. Next lark stood on its tail, driving upwards, the hawk doing the same. The lark lost its bottle and bailed for a group of horses, using their legs for cover. It was probably fortunate that the hawk failed to kill.

Then yet another ringer – the hawk's on top form tonight! She got above it at 400 feet and the lark dropped for a swampy patch with *Why Always Me* on its tail. Arrived to find the merlin on the ground, empty-footed. When I was twenty yards away the lark flushed of its own accord and was taken after a short flight. None of the flights reaching excessive heights tonight, but good sport nonetheless.

September 18

Casper, 193 g. Out again Accrington way with Chris, Rick, Byron, and the two vizslas, Copper *and* Tilly. *A better evening, fine, but a bit breezy.*

First flight at a ground lark, headed downwind, with the merlin flying low and hard. When the lark started to mount she swept round into the wind in a beautiful arc and gained height rapidly. Both birds rang up nicely to 350 feet, where the lark, being hard-pressed, dropped for cover. The hawk was stooping behind as they both disappeared over the brow. We arrived to find her pluming her lark by a dry-stone wall. After a short break we continued, soon putting up another lark that plonked into cover after 30 yards. The merlin stood on the ground a few moments and then took wing again, unimpressed by the close proximity of one of the vizslas, but Rick flushed a lark that 'chirruped' and was away, both birds reaching for the sky. *Casper* almost got a foot to him, lost height and had to drive hard upwards again. The lark went out of sight and very soon I could only just make out the merlin before she was also lost to view. Fortunately Rick and Chris both had field-glasses and were able to give me a running commentary, telling me how the lark suddenly dropped as if bailing for cover but then shot up again, the merlin doing likewise. When the lark dropped a second time, both birds were lost against the hill. Arrived to find the merlin perched on a dry-stone wall and being harassed by a kestrel. A tremendous flight. Fed her up.

September 22

Casper 193 g. Over Accrington, with Allison, Byron, and the vizslas.

First flight a lovely ringer resulting in a vertical stoop down the valley but no kill. Chased a snipe over the horizon but didn't catch it. Next point provided another beautiful ringing flight. A wild merlin joined in, which I thought would ruin things, but *Casper* ignored her and continued her climb into the clear blue sky. When the lark had been lost to view we thought the two hawks had crabbed, but what actually happened was that *Casper* had got a foot to the lark as high as I've ever seen one taken. Maybe the lark having to watch two merlins at once may have had something to do with that.

September 4

Bodmin. Mist and drizzle, coming and going. Why Always Me *183 g.*

Up and down flight across the moor, lots of stoops and throw-ups, not what we're after but a good workout for the hawk – and the lark! Pleased she didn't kill, but then a similar flight did end in a kill. A third such flight ended with the lark bailing for a little flooded boggy hole, no bigger than a dinner-plate. The lark was floating on the water so I tried to photograph it, but it bolted and I had to act as goalkeeper to prevent it coming out and being taken by the hawk. Another point and surprisingly a pipit – wasn't expecting it and let the hawk go. A pretty zig-zagging up and down flight before it was taken. Finally found a good lark that resulted in a ringing flight. The lark drove upwards with the hawk flying off downwind before pumping back into the wind and gaining height until they both started to ring. Could just make out the hawk jinking and stooping before being lost in the mist at 500 feet. Eventually *Why Always Me* came back to the lure. Fed her up.

September 6

Out early on Bodmin with Allison. Why Always Me *187 g. 1400 hours. Scorching hot afternoon. Larks hard to find.*

Eventually got a point, only for the lark to plonk after twenty yards with the merlin landing on the short grass. Before I had a chance to call her back, she spotted it clamped in the grass, ran towards it, and jumped on it! "Oh fiddlesticks!" Or I think that's what I said... Next point and the lark flushed prematurely, flew straight towards me, and was taken a few inches off the ground. "Oh fiddling, fucking frigging sticks!" again. A lot of leg-work before we got another point, which was at least an improvement on the other two! It headed for a herd of cattle where a good old rat-hunt ensued, in and out between the cattle's legs. At one point, unsighted, she sat on a cow. When the lark eventually clamped, with the hawk on the ground nearby, I picked her up and gave the lark a nudge with my foot to flush it, whilst shielding the hawk from sight of it to give it a start. Once again it headed for the cattle but this time, much to my delight, it began to climb. The hawk flew up on her tail, got above it, put in a stoop, and almost caught it at 150 feet. There followed a fantastic ringing flight against the clear blue sky. Up and up they went whilst we sat back to watch the aerial combat, which was right above us as there was hardly a breath of wind. Kept my eyes on the merlin, straining them as she went out of sight and then catching sight of her again as the sunlight glinted, but very briefly, on her wings. Scanning the skies I suddenly caught sight of her again, coming down in a terrific angled stoop. Found her empty-footed on a rock. Fed her up.

September 10

Out with Rich on Moss Moor. Blustery and overcast.

Why Always Me first up. She flew a ground lark which put in successfully, and then commanded a mounter, taking it after a couple of stoops, twists, and turns. Richard's hawk, *Franky*, up next for a decent pipit flight and then one at a good lark but the hawk soon set her wings. Found a good lark for my hawk and she rang up well after it. She was flying at a different level from the lark and it looked at times as if she would throw it but then would continue to beat hard and climb again. The flight was drifting rapidly with the wind and so when I could only just see the merlin I tried to call her in, to no avail. Making my way in the direction of the flight I went over two horizons without a signal. Changed direction, over a third horizon, and still nothing, then the heavens opened. I put the receiver away but took it out occasionally to check for a signal. After much leg-work I trudged back (luring and whistling) to join up with Rich again. He kindly offered to meet me at first light to continue the search, if necessary. Back in the vehicle put my roof-aerial on and after a short drive picked up a faint signal. I parked up as close to the peak signal as I could, and in fading light and persistent rain I stumbled along through the knee-high grass, heather clumps and bogs and hollows and pools of water on the lower slopes. At the end of a race against time I got to the merlin in the dusk, tucked up against a patch of bracken and soaking wet, surrounded by a circle of lark feathers, and with a nice crop. A tough walk back in the darkness on the heavy ground, losing my footing more than once, before a very wet and bedraggled falconer and hawk reached the sanctuary of the van – the hawk I'm sure just as relieved as me. She had been some distance from where I'd last seen her flying. That flight must have been an epic one – I only wished I'd seen it! Back over the M62 for a couple of cold ones in the *Swordfish*.

September 22

Bodmin. Hot and sunny.

Flappy chased a ground lark 100 yards before giving up. Second lark rose and she gave up almost immediately. I had to more or less throw her off at the third lark but she went in the opposite direction and sat on a rock! As well as being useless in the field, her constant bating off the fist is exasperating (and far worse than any spar I've had in the field). Hooded her and headed for home, chuntering to myself that I'd wasted a month of my life. Wouldn't bring her out again. If she were my hawk I'd knock her on the head! Got a point twenty minutes later and thought, "What the hell!" She flew a ground lark down the slope, did a throw-up and a stoop, but the lark made the rushes by the stream so I called her in to the lure. Hmm... at least an improvement. *Marsh* was soon on point again. The lark went straight up and, unbelievably, so did the merlin! I stood open-mouthed. She rang up beautifully to 300 feet before setting her wings. Called her in and fed her up. In the best part of a month in the field, in the process of giving up on easy larks, I don't think she had ever flown higher than 30 feet, if that. I was convinced she suffered from vertigo. One way or another hawks never cease to amaze me.

October 2

Bodmin. Flappy *183 g. Overcast, light breeze.*

First point couldn't have been in a better spot, perfect set-up for a flight and the lark was a good one. The flight looked like being a classic but the merlin set her wings at 200 feet. The second flight was similar except that this time she threw it at 100 feet. Then in a momentary lapse of concentration, I wasn't holding the jesses, she went and caught a pipit, and carried. Luckily, I had made a new lark-stick before setting out, so I was able to pin the quarry and pick her up. The glue hadn't quite set so I now have a lark-stick adorned with pipit feathers. They made it look tribal, or a thing to be used in some kind of pagan ritual. Next a stern twisting course at a ground lark that she killed, and then she got the better of a mounter, flying up on her tail and taking it heading for cover.

October 18

Bodmin. Flappy *183 g. Overcast and breezy.*

First point, and a fine ringing flight, *Flappy* fetching the lark at 600 feet, and followed that with a spectacular zig-zagging stoop as she made slashing cuts at the lark but still failed to kill. If it wasn't for the fact of being in the last few days of the season I should have fed her up. A second similar flight, with the merlin powering upwards, until levelling out to ring. Didn't go as high as the first flight before she sailed back down to the fist, beaten by the lark. Reflushed a ground lark which again didn't go up so didn't bother to reflush it a third time. Several larks rocketed skywards with *Flappy* soon throwing them. A ground lark doubled back and was caught a few feet in front of my face, just as a wild jack came down to investigate, buzzing back and forth over *Flappy*. For the first time in a while managed to pick her up without my stick.

Heading back, got a point and the best flight of the night – the lark lost to view, the hawk drifting in and out of visibility, only occasionally showing a flicker of her wings when, in the clearing weather, the late evening sun would catch her against a dark cloud, before she too was swallowed up in the abyss and I saw no more. I waited before blowing the whistle and she sailed in to the lure. I walked back, feeding her up, revelling in these wonderful surroundings. Time for a quick skate before retiring to the Tavern.

October 20

Last day of the season. Flappy *185 g.*

Pulled up just as another party were coming off the moor having been trying to enter a merlin! One bloke with a whacking great camera and tripod, two pointers *on leads*, merlin not made to the hood dwarfed by a glove a goshawk would have been proud of! Oh, we're a bitchy lot, us falconers.

So, not the best of starts. First lark shot skywards and *Flappy* … sat on a rock. My mood darkened. Several more larks but all with the same result – then, this hawk that had steadfastly refused to bathe, despite an offer of one daily, jumped off a rock and attempted to do just that before I ran over to prevent it. Last day of the season, out on beautiful Bodmin, time to calm down.

She flew a ground lark clean off the moor and returned to the fist. Another lark was marked near some inquisitive cattle. "Now then, my bovine friends," I addressed them, "keep watching, because this is going to be the best flight you've ever seen." (I might have turned out differently if I'd had any friends!). The lark reached for the skies and the hawk swung round and sat on my fist. As Rich would have said, "It is what it is." I took a slow walk back, content with my surroundings and thinking of the sport we've enjoyed over the previous weeks when suddenly I had another point. "Oh well, try again." The merlin went powering up skywards in pursuit of this lark! A lovely ringing flight followed with the lark lost to view at 500 feet but I could see the hawk was still flying hard, by this time off the moor and over a dense plantation. If the lark bailed now the hawk would take some recovering, but she admitted defeat and began sailing down in a long graceful arc back to the fist. A similar flight followed, but not as high, and then as good a pipit flight as you could see, with both birds levelling out at 150 feet for a real ding-dong battle, lots of cuts and slashes, stoops and throw-ups. At first I thought they had merged together but the pipit was the hawk's equal. The flight ended at the bottom of the moor with a fine stoop and throw-up before *Flappy* flew back to the fist. (Why has it taken this hawk all season to fly back to me instead of drifting off to some distant rock and having to be lured?). Next point and the merlin flew straight up with the lark, right on its tail. At 200 feet the hawk veered left to gain height and the lark seized its chance, turned right, and dropped for cover. *Flappy* turned and stooped behind it, slamming into the thick grass at the bottom of the moor, but again failing to kill. When she caught a ground lark putting in, I picked her up alright, and fed her up for the season in the failing light.

Footnote: this hawk only ever caught one lark from a high flight.

September 11

Bodmin.

Put the tiercel up over what turned out to be a false point. Left him up as I tried for another point. A lark bumped wide, and the tiercel gave chase. The lark mounted and *Time Bomb* flew up at 45 degrees, got on terms, and almost got a foot to him. The lark bailed, hawk stooping in its wake. But instead of putting in, the lark rose again and the tiercel stuck with it, onwards and upwards!.

The lark was lost to view, the tiercel, pumping hard was soon out of sight also. He came back into the lure some ten minutes later, beak open. What a fine flight, very reminiscent of Rich's flight with *Maggie* on day one at Ribblehead.

Nasri

September 21

A wet day on Bodmin.

First flight being a nice ringer up to 500 ft, the hawk looking pretty wet and I was sorely tempted to feed her up. However, *Marsh* came on point again and I thought I may as well give it a try. A tail-less lark shot up on its.. err.. tail/arse with *Nasri* in hot pursuit. The hawk gained the ascendancy at 150 ft and the lark began a slanted descent with *Nasri* right on its rear, putting in short stoops as the flight headed down the moor before disappearing over the rise. I arrived at the precipice but could see nothing other than a buzzard flying low across the moor. Suddenly it slammed into the grass and up jumped *Nasri*, saving her life by inches and a split second! I suspected she hadn't caught the lark otherwise she may not have been so lucky. It says something about the mentality of a merlin that I carried on flying her that day, and killed a couple of decent larks.

October 1

Moss Moor, dry and overcast. 0630 hours Nasri *198 g. 1615 hours 183 g.*

Nasri flew a ground lark down the bank, towards the road but fortunately it made cover. Then a repeat of the flight at what I thought was a lark but may well have been a pipit. Saw *Nasri* go into cover right on the verge of the road so was relieved when she came winging her way back to the lure – time to get further out on the moor. Next point was a mounter which *Nasri* got the better of, and a bit of a rat-hunt developed as the hard-pressed lark looked for cover before she caught it. Decided to try over the fence on the other bank.

The next lark was a good one and the hawk did her best up to 200ft but the lark was still rapidly pulling away from her. We both knew that she wasn't going to catch this one and she set her wings. As she came down another lark flushed but as the hawk closed in it plonked. *Nasri* was walking about in the grass looking for the lark which I could see only a couple of feet away from her. Bearing in mind what had happened when she caught her one pipit this season I walked away to call her to the lure, she was a little slow as she wanted the lark.

Another good lark shot skywards, although I thought this one was catchable so major disappointment when *Nasri* gave up on it. I carried on, chuntering to myself about my lazy hawk and deaf dog!

I decided to head back and a lark flushed downwind, the merlin right on its tail. It looked as though she would take the lark easily but jinking over the fence probably saved its life, albeit temporarily. It then shot upwards with *Nasri* on its tail. Both birds levelled out and began to ring, the classic *haut vol*. No sign of *Nasri* giving up on this one, wings still pumping hard and by the time they reached 500ft I was praying she would catch this one. Suddenly I saw the lark drop a little and a wild jack appeared from nowhere and took the lark. *Nasri*, obviously not best pleased with this impudent intruder stealing her lunch, gave chase. She got in a couple of short stoops which the jack avoided but on the third stoop she bound to him. I thought she would let him go again, but no, down they came over the brow and lost to view. I raced across the moor, arriving at the spot where I thought they had come down but no sign. I got the receiver out and found *Nasri* sitting on her lark, no sign of the jack. He had obviously given up the lark to save his bacon! *Nasri*'s highest flight to date ending in a kill, albeit via a third party. Don't think I'll be flying in a cast at the Ribblehead meet this weekend.

October 6

Ribblehead field meet.

A good lark and nice looking flight developing, but, to audible groans from the field *Nasri* set her wings at less than 200 ft. A wild jack then appeared on the scene to take up the chase. This suddenly reinvigorated *Nasri* who immediately changed gear and resumed the flight. This was shaping up into a good flight but was about to get even better as a wild merlin joined the fray. The poor lark, now seriously outnumbered, made a valiant effort to continue to trust his wings, before it all got too much for him, and he bailed for cover with a triumvirate of merlins stooping in his wake. Soon enough the falling lark and merlins were swallowed up in the moor. I ran over, and when I was about 50 yards from the spot where they had come down, the wild merlin jumped up and exited stage left. No sign of the jack, *Nasri* sitting on her lark. But was it hers? Had she taken it fair and square or robbed one of her wild cousins? We will never know.

Seriously Outnumbered

October 14

Breezy and warm on Bodmin, Colliford, Heather out. Nasri *186 g.*

Nasri turned tail on the first lark, *Marsh* snapped up the second one! Then a good lark and a good flight, the hawk flying straight to

the lark, climbing at 60 degrees and reaching parity at 200 ft. Both birds then rung up another hundred feet before the hard-pressed lark bailed, with *Nasri* stooping behind it but she failed to kill. With it being the last week of the season and a lot of fully moulted larks grouping together I thought about feeding her up, which I would have done if she'd taken the lark.

Flushed a mounter and *Nasri* was all over it. I thought she had him putting in but he got up again and they both disappeared from view down towards the plantation off the bottom of the moor. She didn't return so assumed she had caught it, but as I neared the plantation I was getting all sorts of interference on the receiver so had to walk back up the moor to get a signal. The signal was coming from the other end of the plantation, which I thought was strange. Followed it off the moor, up the slope, a good signal now but what on earth was she doing over here? Then I lost the signal completely.

I walked to a high point and picked up a faint signal back towards the wood. Made my way down, and although I was getting a good signal I was in and out of the edge of the wood and couldn't seem to pinpoint it. I then got a banging signal on, near where a buzzard jumped up with something in its feet, it flew to the wood and landed in the trees and the signal grew weaker.

As I approached it, and it left the trees, the signal grew stronger again, I was now fearing the worst. The buzzard was now joined by two more buzzards, and after a bit of a skirmish they all flew off, empty-footed. I pinpointed the signal to the branches above me, climbed a tree with a buzzard's nest in it, and then saw what was left of *Nasri*, in the branches of an adjacent tree. Retrieved the dead hawk, the buzzard had eaten half her head, breast, and plucked her tail and one wing.

I presume *Nasri* had taken her lark on the edge of the plantation, and the opportunistic buzzard, sitting in the trees, had dropped onto the unsuspecting hawk. It's hard to express the feeling of having your hawk so tragically taken from you. I think having a merlin killed in the field hits harder than losing any other type of hawk. This is because it's such an intense, short season, for eight weeks or so your whole life is taken over, all day every day, by the welfare of your tiny

Outnumbered

hawk. The diligence required in feeding and weighing, weathering and offering a bath, which unlike other hawks requires the falconer in attendance. All life is geared up towards the afternoon or evening on the moor, then when the hawk is placed in the mews for the night the falconer can relax until dawn the following day. Every waking hour is consumed by the lark hawking season for the merlin-man.

The Curse of Colliford

As a footnote to *Nasri* being killed at Colliford, another disaster has occurred at this location before going to press so I thought it worth recording.

Running a little short of time I thought I would just fly *Time Bomb*, the tiercel, to the kite. However I'd parked up by a likely looking boggy field so figured it was worth giving the dog a run, perchance of a snipe. Walked it up but found nothing so was heading back to the van to get the kite. A snipe suddenly jumped (missed on the way down by the dog!), flew a few yards then put in. Closer than I would have liked to the A30 but I figured it wouldn't come into play.

Put the hawk up and waited for him to gain his pitch. Road-side of the snipe I sent *Marsh* in but nothing flushed. Waited whilst the tiercel put in another ring, drifting wide, but the snipe flushed leading to an angled stoop. Instead of heading out across the fields, as I had expected, the snipe headed in the direction of the road. Hawk and snipe disappeared from view, far too close to the road for comfort. I clambered up the small bank to see the snipe dead in the road, and on the opposite carriageway, the tiercel on his back at the side of the road. I picked up the snipe and bundled the tiercel under my arm, at that moment to be joined by *Marsh* who had been instructed to wait in the field. God only knows how she had made it across four lanes without being run over herself. Once back in the field the tiercel began to struggle, he was still alive! I stood him on the fist and he seemed alright in himself but had a bald patch on his head where he had been hit and severe damage to his right eye, which, at the time of writing looks lost. Hindsight is a wonderful thing.

To lure or not to lure…?

There has been a fair bit of discussion amongst the merlin men in recent times, as to the merits of getting the hawk fit before entering, by spending a couple of weeks stooping to the lure. So, for what its worth, I may as well add my two-penn'orth!

Myself and Rich are not the only two merlin men who get their hawks flying free, then head to the marsh looking for suitable quarry on which to enter her. A young or heavily moulting lark, or even a lark that goes up a 100ft or so before bailing for cover are all within the hawks capabilities. Basically, every day on the moor, the hawk is flown fit. After a few easy larks to learn the game so the standard of flight and the hawks fitness increase. I don't hold with the statement that an unfit hawk will be beaten by a strong lark and that will put her off trying to take them the rest of the season. We need to credit the hawk with a little bit of nous at this point. At the end of the season the merlin may refuse half a dozen larks in a row, then go like her life depends on it at the 7th lark which puts up, although to the human eye the lark looks no different than the previous six. The merlin knows in an instant if she thinks she has a chance of catching it, in the same way as she does early in the season when she is not yet at full fitness.

There have been some star hawks trained in this way, just as there have been star hawks which have been stooped to the lure.

Stop Press

Just when you thought you had met with just about every possible disaster, life throws up a new one!

Up in the Highlands, flying *Simon*, a very promising looking first-year tiercel. He was a little bit above himself having been fed up on grouse for a few consecutive days. We'd already had two flights but he had failed to kill. One more point and call it a day, methinks.

Marsh on point, *Simon* up, made his pitch, but was slightly out of position so I waited. He began to drift with the breeze, losing interest in proceedings. I called and waved the glove but to no avail. Nothing else for it but to call him down. He immediately began pumping hard to the lure, driving down at an angle when suddenly he just fell out of the sky, followed a second or two later by an audible thud. He had been cut down by a wind turbine propeller. Must be a million to one chance. The propeller had come down just at the base of his back, killing him instantly. Poor *Simon* is buried up on the moor – what a great hawk he would have become.

CHAPTER SEVEN

Food for Thought

FALCONRY TODAY IS practised purely for the sport it provides, and no longer for putting food on the table, certainly not in the West. Despite this every effort should be made to put the body of the vanquished quarry to good use. I abhor profligacy in any form, and so, regardless of the species of quarry taken I always try to utilise it to the full, whether as food for human, hawk, dog, or ferret, wings for lures, feathers for fishing-flies or even just for decoration. Using quarry in this way is relatively straightforward for the austringer with a goshawk. No goshawker worth his or her salt is going to let rabbits and game-birds go to waste, and will find a use for squirrels or moorhens. The game-hawker is, of course, thoroughly spoilt, but few crow-hawkers are inclined to dine on their quarry (probably with good reason) and fewer still among the gull and lark-hawkers. This is actually surprising in the case of the lark-hawkers, since the lark was traditional fare (as passerines still are in countries outside the UK) and was not eaten just by falconers.

During the 1920s, as the dying embers of the O.H.C. made way for the green shoots of the B.F.C., the small remaining band of falconers would have an annual meeting in London for a 'falconers feast,' with lark and oyster pie being one of the highlights of the menu. The present-day lark-hawker is at a slight disadvantage since the annual licence issued by Natural England allows for the taking of only fifteen larks during the season – hardly enough to fill a decent pie! However, I am lucky enough to be able to embellish my catch with larks from other merlin-men with less discerning palates. An eagerly awaited pleasure of this unique branch of the sport is dining on larks at the close of the season. It is a beautiful, rich, dark meat. Since it happens only once a year, and is a very rare privilege, I always make the most of it. By the end of the season I usually manage to acquire fifty or sixty frozen larks that haven't been fed to the merlins. From their breasts and offal there is enough for a meal for myself and a couple of friends.

By contrast, gulls are available for the best part of six months of the year, and a gull, quite obviously, stretches a little further than a skylark. It provides a rich dark meat very similar to a prime cut of beef with a slight gamey flavour. It's amazing how many people will refuse to eat gull without even tasting it, just because of what it is. Most people in this country have a misconception that meat is shrink-wrapped and comes from cow, sheep, pig, or chicken (plus turkey once a year) and anything else is taboo. Many people who have been to my house and steadfastly refused to eat gull or crow have done just that, albeit unknowingly, usually in a bolognaise or a casserole. I usually eat just first-year gulls, the meat being more tender than that of the adults (which I use predominantly for hawk-food, although I will sometimes use them for mince). I don't hang gulls, as one would a pheasant, but birds for the table have generally been used as lures for a few of days, as advocated by the late, great Stephen Frank when preparing grouse for the table.

Given the choice I prefer gull to corvid, although a good rook-pie has been a regular on the menu over the years. Gull breast, trimmed and seasoned, can be substituted for best steak, and is an ideal addition to a cooked breakfast if not used for a main meal.

Although not strictly running with the themes of the book, a couple of additional recipes would not, I think, go amiss.

Squirrel Chilli Pancakes

Some austringers purposefully fly their hawks at squirrels but most look on them just as sundries. However, *Tufty* the tree rat (although *Tufty* the TV star was actually a red squirrel, which is definitely not on the menu these days), is easily procured with the use of an air-rifle.

Batter:	*Plain flour*	*Eggs*
	Milk	*Salt*

Filling:	*Squirrels (one per person)*	
	Chillis	*Pepper*
	Red onion	*Salt, Black pepper*

Dressing:	*Mayonaisse, Garlic, Crème fraiche, Grain mustard*

Garnish:	*Chilli flakes, Paprika, Lemon*

Prepare the batter-mix for the pancakes, leave in the fridge for an hour before making up the pancakes (Shop-bought wraps may be used as an alternative).

Skin the squirrels (they should have been gutted immediately after being killed) and remove the leg-meat and saddles, and liver, kidneys, and heart (if offal is to your taste). Slice the meat into strips, and seal it for a minute in a frying pan with seasoned extra virgin olive oil. Remove from pan and place to one side.

Slice the peppers, chillis, and onion, and sauté in the same pan, adding seasoning and paprika. Warm the pancakes in the grill or microwave. Add the squirrel to the pan to heat through, and then fill the pancakes before adding the dressing which is made up of the ingredients listed, with a squeeze of lemon juice, a dusting of paprika, chilli flakes, and chopped parsley.

Just a word of warning about eating squirrel and that is: Don't eat too many. If you do you may develop a craving for nuts and shinning up trees.

Sweet and Sour Rabbit

1 Rabbit (serves 2 to 3)
1 Jar sweet and sour sauce
Pilau rice
Plain flour
Salt, black pepper

Skin the rabbit, remove the meat (including offal) from the bone and cut into mouth-size bites and season with salt and black pepper. Make up a basic batter with the plain flour and water and season with salt. Add the meat to the batter. Heat the oil in a deep-fat fryer and put in as many pieces of batter-covered meat as you can fit in without them sticking together. When each piece is golden and floating in the oil remove and place in kitchen-roll, repeating until all the rabbit pieces have been cooked. Cook the rice and heat the sweet and sour. Drop the pieces back into the oil for a few seconds just to heat them up and crisp the batter. Place the pieces on the rice. Spoon over the sweet and sour.

You can of course make your own sweet and sour, but using a jar makes this a very quick and easy meal to prepare.

Lark And Kidney Pie

Larks (50)	*Shortcrust pastry*
Lamb's kidneys (4)	*Beef stock*
Red onion	*Red wine*
Carrots	*Salt, black pepper, herbs*
Leek	

Throughout the season all your larks, and those scrounged from your friends, will of course have been stored in the freezer. Incidentally, I feed only the head and neck of a lark to the merlin – hence the remainder of the carcass being still intact.

First comes the fiddly time-consuming part: removing all the breasts, livers, and hearts from the defrosted larks and ensuring all the meat is free from small feathers – unless you require some casting with your pie. Cut the lamb's kidneys into chunks about equivalent in size to four or five lark's breasts. Marinade the meat in seasoned extra virgin olive oil with a splash of red wine for an hour or two.

With this being a once-a-year meal I prefer to make my own pastry, but shortcrust pastry is obviously available from the supermarkets.

Roll out the pastry for the pie-base and pre-cook in a greased Pyrex dish weighed down with dried chick-peas on top of grease-proof paper.

Chop the vegetables, add the stock and red wine, the seasoning and herb of choice, and cook slowly, either on the stove or in a slow-cooker until the veg is tender but not soggy. Whilst this is cooking, seal the lark and kidney for a minute in a pan with a little extra virgin olive oil. Remove from the pan and place to one side.

When the veg is done add the meat and pour into the pie-base, roll out the pastry for the lid. Once on, crimp it and make three slits for ventilation. Brush with egg-yolk and place in a hot, pre-heated oven for 20-25 minutes until the pie is golden.

Serve with new potatoes and broccoli.

Roast Woodcock

I must confess that I can count the number of woodcock that I have caught with hawks on one hand, an incidental flight for short and long wings alike. Top of my culinary list of game birds, it is the only species that I will actually buy.

Preparation: Plume the woodcock and remove the gizzard, leaving the head, pushing the beak back through the body acting as a skewer.

Heat a frying pan containing a little extra virgin oil and seal the 'cock. Place in a pre-heated oven at 170 degrees for 30 minutes, being careful not to over-cook.

Whilst the bird rests, make a piece of fried bread in the frying pan. Spoon the innards out of the woodcock, mash it into the fried bread, a squeeze of lemon or lime juice and sit the bird on top.

This process can be repeated for snipe (reducing the cooking time) which is a very close second to woodcock.

Seagull Stir-fry

If like me you now live in camper-van* and spend the winter months hawking gulls (where have you gone wrong in life?) then the seagull stir-fry becomes pretty much your staple winter diet.

Apart from a couple of thickly-sliced gulls' breasts (and the offal), a red onion, and soy sauce, it's usually just a case of whatever I've got to hand in the van, salad, chillis, spinach, and even beansprouts if I've been really extravagant in the shops. Basically, it's all just tossed in the pan over the gas-bottle for a couple of minutes and Robert's your mother's brother.

As a footnote to living in a camper-van, the following story may be of interest.

I had been living in my van, a stealth camper, for over a year, my only form of heat being candles. Every time I saw or spoke to Nick he would ask me the same question, 'Have you got yourself a carbon monoxide detector for that van yet?' To which he always received the same answer,

'No, not got round to it yet, but it is on my to do list'.

Visiting Nick one weekend he placed a package on the kitchen table, 'There, I've got you one, you owe me £20. Then knowing full well that it would probably remain in the box, he kindly fitted it for me.

That was on Saturday. On Tuesday, in the early hours, I was fast asleep when I was suddenly woken by the ear piercing alarm of the carbon monoxide detector. I had not blown my candles out, they had overheated the ceramic pot and the lino on which they stood was smouldering, close to flames. My van was full of smoke, so I leaped out and was left standing in the supermarket car park in my boxers, all the doors to my van open, smoke billowing out.

Nick had pretty much saved my life and more importantly the lives of four hawks and a dog.

Hawking Hostelries

Listed here are a few of the public houses where I have enjoyed a post-hawking or between-flights pint.

The Swordsman (*now the New Inn*)
Stamford Bridge,
York

The Bay Horse
Stamford Bridge
York

The Carpenters Arms
Fangfoss
York

The Agar Arms
Warthill
York

The Kingfisher (*now closed*)
Holme-upon-Spalding
York

The Ship Inn (*now closed*)
Moor Skiptonthorpe
York

The Rose and Crown
Askham Richard
York

The Tankard
Rufforth
York

The Sun
Acomb
York

The Red Lion
Upper Poppleton
York

The Triton
Sledmere
Driffield

The Bell
Tamworth-in-Arden
Warwickshire

The Boot
Nr Studley
Warwickshire

The Forsinard Hotel
Forsinard
Sutherland

The Grey Horse
Elvington
York

Riggers Bar (*now closed*)
Alness
Invernesshire

The Balconnie Hotel
Evanton
Invernesshire

The Plough
Sutton Courtenay
Oxfordshire

The Augustus John
Fordingbridge
Hampshire

The Colliford Tavern
Colliford Lake
Bodmin
Cornwall

The Park
Accrington
Lancashire

Rose and Crown
Tilshead
Wiltshire

Commercial Hotel
Alness
Scotland

Halfway House
Bodmin
Cornwall (*Great food*)

The Rockingham Arms
Towton
North Yorkshire

The Moor and Pheasant
Dalton
North Yorkshire

The Kings Head
Five Lanes
Launceston
Cornwall

The Queens Head
St Stephen
St Austell
Cornwall

Rams Head
Denshaw
Saddleworth

Jamaica Inn
Bodmin
Cornwall

The Rod and Line
Tideford
Cornwall

FALCON RULES – O.K.

by Ken McKinley

Man and bird together in perfect harmony
Have learnt respect and trust for everyone to see.
Step by step and slowly
A life of faith they span
To have a bond and loyalty
A part of Nature's plan

Now people say birds should be free
To live their life to the full
Not tethered to a bow at night
Or hooded from the sun

Now they will never know the thrill
Or sights they may have missed
To see a falcon take its prey
Or a gos slipped from the fist

Some people hunt with shotguns
With rods fish through the night
But nothing is more deadly
Than a falcon in full flight

If some could make the time it takes
To fly a bird of prey
Then they would know the skill it needs
An art from day to day

Now hawks and falcons can be trained
But never will be tame
The bird will always know what's best
And you're the one to blame

Don't think you're in control
With whistle lure and line
As I have said the falcon knows
And she wins every time!

CHAPTER EIGHT

Correspondence – *Beccy, Polack et al*

EACH SEASON WE collect our merlins from Nick. We're all hoping for that star bird. Truth be told there is never a 'duffer,' just some better than others. Even hawks that we end up disappointed with, I've not known one yet that fails to show any sport, all at some stage provide the ringing flight, it's just they are far less consistent. The best of them provide regular/daily ringing flights. Then there is the very best, the star birds that come along once in a blue moon, hawks that go through the season rarely beaten, excellent footers, and an absolute pleasure to fly. It always makes us think about our own methods, have we done something different in training or in the field to reach this Elysium? Truth be told, no, it is down to the hawk.

Casper was one such merlin. Still to this day the best merlin I have ever had, or indeed ever seen. She was a star amongst star hawks. Her first lark was a prelude to things to come, no ground lark or yellow belly. It was at RAF Leeming with Nick. A good mounter, and although the hawk reached parity with it at 200ft the lark was still intent on outflying the hawk, but this novice merlin was its equal. The lark bailed and the hawk got a foot to him before he reached the ground. I couldn't tell but Nick, with better eyesight than me said, *"she's got that."* I was a little sceptical but sure enough Nick was right. Still the best 'first kill' I've had with a merlin.

A week later, again at Leeming I'd given her the head and neck of a lark and almost immediately a good lark flushed and she soon set her wings. That was the last time she ever did so. This merlin had everything you could ever wish for in a hawk. When it saw a lark it just wanted to catch it, and didn't stop until it had done so or the lark had bailed and made cover. In addition to her tremendous mental attitude was her superb footing, flying skills and stamina.

September 30

A dry, bright afternoon but a strong wind. Was going to go to Moss Moor but then, for a change decided to try Rishworth Moor. Once on there the ground didn't seem so good, thicker heather, some bracken. A long walk and not a lark in sight (*Chaos* useless). A pipit flushed. Shit! My reactions were too slow (must be getting old) and I'd inadvertently let the hawk go and she'd killed it. Never mind, onwards and upwards. Eventually a lark flushed (had *Chaos* with me), a good one, just what we were after. A tremendous flight ensued; as good as it gets against the clear blue sky. As well as the colossal height the flight was attaining it was also drifting in the strong wind. The last I saw of it was the merest flicker of the merlin's wings, caught by the sun, still pumping hard after her lark. I followed in the direction, a mile or more but the signal was still weak. Carry on walking or back to the van? A short deliberation, then I chose the latter. I never got a signal again, nor was *Casper* ever seen or heard of again. I trudged the moors for the best part of two weeks, but nothing. I was kicking myself for flying such a good hawk in the wind. I put it to the merlin-men that if you have a hawk that good it shouldn't be flown on windy days, because if you get a good lark the flight could potentially finish a long way off. It was at least a small crumb of comfort that to a man they disagreed. It's a short season as it is and for the amount of windy days you have on northern moorland, if you didn't fly you may as well not bother flying a merlin at all (perhaps take up Crown Green Bowling?).

It is such a shame she was lost before the end of the season. I would love to have seen her take on a fully moulted lark. In hindsight I suppose she was always destined to be lost as the very best hawks often are. A microcosm of the highest highs and lowest lows of the sport – a fantastic, memorable flight followed by the loss of the hawk.

Which brings us to *Beccy*, another exceptional merlin flown by Richard Waddington. I will let him tell the story in his own words by reproducing emails he has sent to Nick, describing some of the sport he enjoyed. But first, a short description of one of *Beccy's* flights by Nick:

It falls to me to recount the best flight Richard ever had, for the archives. Not being there, the task is somewhat difficult, but I will give it a go. Richard phoned to tell me, as he said it was too spectacular to put down into words. He was out on the moor with our wonderful photographer Chris. Up gets a lark and immediately puts in. Richard rightly surmised it was a good lark and decides to re-flush – after all, it was just a short flight not a 'proper' one. He stands around with Chris talking for ten minutes to let Beccy *settle, before flying again. They go forward to flush the lark and a pipit gets up.* Beccy *is off in a flash and a very exciting flight follows, but she eventually give up and returns to Richard. Todd knows the lark is still there and another five minutes elapses, while* Beccy *recovers her breath, before they hunt the lark again. Up gets the lark and the flight is on. Up, up and up they go,* Beccy *is not letting this one get away, eventually Richard can see them no more. Chris can still see them through his binoculars, but eventually even he can only make out the merlin.* Beccy *was all over this lark, it wasn't getting away. She brought her lark down and Richard picked her up a mile away. She was sat on the edge of a road. The lark had escaped. Richard fed her up and was just glad she hadn't caught a car instead. They only ever manage to catch one car in a lifetime.*

It sounded a lot more exciting than that on the phone, with various "Bloody hell Chris, have you ever seen anything like that before" and much more.

A poor effort on my part, but we can all imagine the bits in between, the start and finish of the flight, by previous descriptions from Richard, which I could never better. This merlin is turning into something special. We are all scared to say too much in case we jinx the whole show. We are all holding our breath for the next instalment.

And now for Richard's email correspondence. (These are unedited, so as not to lose Richard's obvious passion for the flight).

Hi Nick,

Well I don't know what to say really, what I do know is I've never seen a merlin like this [*Richard never saw* Casper *fly*] I'm sure the boys down country have, but not up here. This merlin is the best we've had 'in my time anyway'. We had two flights tonight, I mean two flights, flights that could not be equalled. The first flight was high, I mean high, really high, the lark bailed and *Beccy* was on this lark. Chris and I had lark and merlin in a fantastic stoop through the binoculars, when that damn peregrine came out of a stoop and hit the merlin. "What the bloody hell is going on," shouted Chris, all I could think was, "*Beccy!!*" I set off looking for my special merlin. I didn't have to go far, Beccy was looking for me, my thoughts, she came up the moor and landed on my fist. We sat down for a while and went through the flight, ten times. I decided to go for another. *Todd* worked this lark for an age, bang! Point. Get in! Lark up, a good lark and a good merlin. The flight was well and truly on. I had the merlin, Chris had the lark in the binoculars, up, up, up, they went, it was just one massive ring, with the merlin pumping and pumping. I watched the merlin take her chance and shouted to Chris, "keep on the lark, *Beccy* is on her way", or something similar. *Beccy* was on this lark high in the sky, stoop after stoop, trying to force her lark down all the time. If you had no binoculars you would have missed this flight. After a series of stoops the lark bailed out, down they went with no throw up. Yes I thought, she's got this lark. I was wrong, she had lost her lark in a farm-yard. Ah well, I fed her up, and home time.

Many thanks,
Richard

P.S. The only way that flight could have been bettered, was with a kill. There is plenty left in this merlin, Nick!

This picture is where the peregrine hit *Beccy*, you can see the feet still down, they both came down to earth, but *Beccy* must have out

Enemy at the rear

manoeuvred the peregrine, she must have or she would not be here.
Many thanks,
Richard

P.S. You must remember all these pictures taken with a 500 prime with a 1.4 converter and a crop factor of 1.3 which in all comes to about mmmmmmmmmmm ... a lot.

Hi Nick,
Today was just unbelievable. The first flight was on a common snipe, heavy in moult, it was just like flying a ground lark, but faster. I could not believe it when the merlin bound to it. Chris said, "Now that's one for the diary." The second flight was a decent flight on lark that went up, but came down straight away. *Beccy* took this lark. After that we flew two more larks that just wouldn't go up. *Beccy* took them both. On the day we ended up with three larks and a snipe.
They weren't the flights we wanted. I would have settled for one

good ringing flight, but that is just how the day went and the merlin did its job well. I don't like taking larks like that, but you can't make them go up.

Many thanks,

Richard

Not a sight you see every day of the week

Hi Nick,

Had one good flight, that's all we needed. The merlin got on this lark, she wanted it, but the lark wasn't going to make it easy. They both made their way up into the clouds. I'll bet it was two minutes before *Beccy* made her first swipe at her lark. The best thing about this flight was it all happened right above our heads and you could see everything. *Beccy* never missed a wing beat, neither did the lark. The lark gave in first and a breathtaking stoop unfolded. Everything above our heads, fantastic to watch. She caught her lark, I was made up. Fed her up, home time.

Many thanks,

Richard

Hi Nick,

Beccy had her work cut out tonight. Plenty of larks on the hill. A lot of these larks are passing through, they always do at this time of year. These larks where strong, very strong. *Beccy* flew three and caught one. The first flight was on a very strong lark and *Beccy* struggled to get to terms with it. They both went high, Chris and I watched them through binoculars. *Beccy* set her wings, the flight was over. The second lark got up under my feet. It was fully moulted and went like a train. This lark went straight up singing all the way. *Beccy* made a half-hearted attempt and set her wings. The third flight was a ringing flight, but you could just tell the lark wasn't as good as the previous larks and boy *Beccy* knew it. This lark was in trouble all the way, but fair play to the lark, it stayed high while *Beccy* was chopping at it. The lark bailed with the merlin on its tail. I picked the merlin up, with her lark in a farm-yard.

Many thanks,
Richard

P.S. A bitter sweet night. Every year is the same at this time on the hill, you get these tooled up larks passing through.

The bitter sweet moment is knowing the end of the season is nigh. Richard finished flying soon after this and *Beccy* was returned to Nick to hopefully breed new generations of high flying merlins.

Well I've already mentioned the infrequency of those star hawks, and then Richard has two in the same year! By the way, although these hawks are exceptional they still need to be in capable hands. It does help if you happen to be a bloody good falconer, and Richard is certainly that.

So at the end of his best ever lark hawking season Richard acquired a tiercel peregrine, *Polack*, to be flown at snipe on the high northern moors. The sport he has obtained is of the highest calibre, different again from the lowland snipe hawking, not that that is not good sport in its own right. This super-fit, super-persevering, super-fast Exocet missile of a hawk has to be seen to be believed. Then add to this the local peregrines joining in with the flights on a daily basis and we thought it couldn't get any better. When watching a flight at snipe with *Polack* and the wild tiercel you can't tell one from the other, which is as high a compliment as I can pay to *Polack*.

Once *Polack* was down for the season, Richard and Chris continued to go out on the moor with the dogs, the wild tiercel waiting on over them, having fine flights and taking snipe just like a trained hawk, fortunately all captured on video.

Anyway once again I will relate some of the sport via Richard's emails to Nick.

Hi Nick

We never flew yesterday – the weather was brutal. We walked a bit and a common jumped and put back in about a hundred yards away. This was the snipe we wanted, hood off, rouse, away *Polack*, went straight up to a good height. *Polack* came round and was directly over us – I was shaking, I knew what was coming. Get in *Todd*! Snipe up. *Polack* was coming down, he missed on the stoop. The flight that followed made my hair curl. The snipe made its way to a plantation and wanted to bail, but *Polack* was stuck to this snipe, in and out of the plantation, fast and furious. *Polack* wanted this snipe. The pressure was too much for the snipe and the only way out was to go high. The flight had only just started. It was like a merlin on a lark, but higher. The snipe would pull thirty, forty yards and you would think, well that's it then. *Polack* is just relentless, Nick. I watched every bit of this flight through the binoculars and was giving Chris a running commentary. You could just see little jinks and the snipe pulling and then *Polack* back again and again. I could not believe what I was watching. The snipe was well out of view now and you could just see *Polack* twisting and turning and then the big stoop. The snipe had bailed. Both *Polack* and snipe had gone, where God only knew. Telemetry out and tracking we must go. To cut a long story short, we found *Polack* on St Mary's Chambers, a court house in Rawtenstall, a town about four miles away from where he was slipped. I swung my lure in the town centre and *Polack* came

Down we go

straight down to it, nobody was any the wiser. I was so happy to get *Polack* back on my fist, he had missed his snipe. That flight, Nick, was the best flight I have ever witnessed with a trained falcon. This tiercel is so focused.

Many thanks,
Richard

5/11/2014

Hi Nick,

We have been watching some real sport lately, Nick. All of the stoops have been from high pitches. *Polack* is one very fit tiercel and there are plenty of snipe on the moor.

Today was something different. We had a point and I unhooded him, *Polack* flew out of sight looking for lift and as usual he came over very high. Then it all went tits up, as the local peregrines came in and took *Polack* up high into the clouds. *Polack* at one point hit

133

Catch me if you can

the female peregrine, she is a brown bird, they eventually got fed up of each other and *Polack* came over. We got a fantastic stoop and he pushed the common hard. The snipe bailed to a pond and made cover. *Polack* went straight back up. I wanted to reflush this snipe, as he hasn't had a kill for a couple of days. Just as *Polack* was coming round, the local tiercel flew right underneath him, on the back of a pigeon. Well, the flight that followed was, well … *Polack* came thundering down and joined in the flight. The poor pigeon did not stand a chance, both *Polack* and the wild peregrine were taking swipes at it. I watched *Polack* take this pigeon right in front of the wild one, (you do need those binoculars) I was buzzing. I picked him up a mile away on his pigeon. From unhooding *Polack* to him taking the pigeon, he was on the wing 45 minutes.

On the way back myself and Young Chris were talking about the flight, when *Todd* locked up. I thought it was a jack and Chris thought common. We where both wrong, a woodcock jumped, the first one of the season. I was just thinking I would love to get a chance to fly a woodcock and then out of the blue came the wild tiercel. I could hardly believe what I was watching, he must have been waiting on above us. This tiercel meant business, he was all over the woodcock, probably due to losing the pigeon to *Polack*. The flight was soon over, he took his woodcock in front of us. Myself and Chris were both a bit stunned. The flight finished in a ground flight across the moor twisting and turning. That woodcock was going nowhere. The wild tiercel made the day. You can only dream of having a bird as fit as that. We watched the tiercel carry the woodcock at least two mile back to the local quarry.

Many thanks,

Richard

The Wild Tiercel Day, written up by Nick Ellison

16/11/2014

Chris, Young and Old and myself out with Richard. Polack a little high at 1lb 6.

Up at a decent height, but we couldn't find the snipe; eventually it flushed with the hawk out of position, so a long slanting stoop which the quarry evaded. So too the second stoop, followed by *Polack* chasing it into the distance, before coming back overhead. We found another snipe, with the hawk at a good pitch, a cracking stoop, basically the same result as the first flight. Back over he came, another snipe, stoop and it put in. Flushed it again with the same result. Up went *Polack* again, snipe put up, *Polack* stooped and again it ended with the hawk flying it into the distance, putting it in. *Polack* came back over, Rich tried the lure, no chance! *Polack* was now joined by a wild tiercel, which didn't faze him. Another snipe, this one put in and up went the hawk yet again. Rich tried the lure again, ha. Another snipe which flew low, hoodwinking the hawk (and humans) that it was going to drop in, making *Polack* pull out of the stoop. The snipe then rose rapidly, powering away, *Polack* in hot pursuit. Suddenly the wild tiercel joined in, overtaking his trained counterpart, he was all over the snipe, almost getting a foot to him. There can't be a fitter trained hawk in Britain than *Polack*, but it just goes to show what the wild hawk is capable of. The snipe knew he was in serious trouble and headed for cover, all three birds lost to view. Tracked *Polack* down off the moor into the valley and a couple of fields away. There was *Polack* on his very well deserved snipe. What a hawk!!

28/11/2014

Hi Nick,

What a day! We went on a different part of the Lord's moor today – I hope he's OK with that. Dog on point, *Polack* away and getting high. He came round into position, I was just getting ready to flush and Chris shouted, "That bloody peregrine is here again." Today was different though, both birds where tolerating each other and both peregrines were directly above us. Get in *Todd*! Snipe up and both tiercels coming down at speed. This snipe was in big trouble, it just had to bail, which it did and it saved its life. Both wild peregrine and *Polack* were soon back over and waiting for their next slip. Bang, dog on point. Both birds at a good height. Chris said, "Which one's *Polack*?" I said, "Who cares? Get in!" Both tiercels came down side by side in amazing stoops, one bend, snipe bailed. You can't blame the snipe, after all it is their life. We had four flights with *Polack* and the wild one, without any bird landing and both birds flying off the moor and then coming back over. I pulled *Polack* in to the lure and fed him up. I was proud of my little tiercel.

Sam, Chris's new pup, was locked up on point. Well, not a pup, about twelve months old. Anyway, the wild tiercel was above us again, this bird does not give up. Get in! The flight was on and what a flight, up, up, up, the flight went, until we could not see anymore, the tiercel pumping all the way. He missed his snipe, because he was back over us five minutes later, waiting for another flight. *Todd* was on a runner and I knew it was there. I blew him down and waited for the tiercel to get in position. Nick, it was like flying a trained falcon. He came round at about 200 ft, he didn't need to be any higher, to be honest you don't need a high flying hawk to catch snipe. Get in! Snipe up and tiercel coming down. The flight that followed was mind-blowing, Nick. If you remember, about a month ago Nick, I sent you an email about the best flight I have ever had with a trained falcon, well that was beat hands down. Both myself and Chris where gobsmacked. We didn't see the wild one again, I'm sure he had his snipe, I hope so, he definitely deserved it. All in all we had eight flights at common snipe with *Polack* and the wild tiercel with no kill seen. You must commend those snipe, what a cracking little bird and a great test for a wild, or trained falcon alike. The best flights to be had at common snipe are on the high moors of the North, without a doubt. A truly amazing day, and one we will never forget.

Many thanks,

Richard

4/12/2014

Hi Nick,

I took *Polack* out, too high in weight and I had a few problems. Anyway, we are back on track now. Today was a red letter day for sure. I decided to put *Polack* up without a point and walk onto the moor. I knew there were going to be snipe on the hill, despite the frosty night. *Polack* was at a nice height, I couldn't believe it, the wild tiercel had only brought his wife to join in the fun. *Todd* was locked up with *Sam* backing him, Chris's new dog. All three falcons high and in position. Nick, all three peregrines knew what was coming. I said to Chris, "Are you ready for this," laughing. Get in! Snipe up and all three peregrines coming down at this little snipe. *Polack* was the first to bend the snipe, the reason being *Polack* was in a better position. He threw up, then the wild tiercel came in and almost took the snipe. It was very confusing, Nick, it was happening very fast. *Polack* came in for the second time and took the snipe. It was pay back for the other day. I fed my tiercel up on the snipe, hood on and we were making off the hill. Chris then said, "Here look, both wild ones are waiting on above us, lets get them a slip." Dog on. Get in! Both wild ones coming down. This was the flight of the day, both falcon and tiercel taking turns, you could see they were working as a team. The tiercel caught this snipe very high up and gave it to the falcon on the wing. The tiercel came straight back over waiting for another flush. We found him another four flights at snipe, which he flew into the heavens, ringing them up just like merlin and lark, but he never looked in control without the falcon at his side. He didn't catch any we put up for him. How good are those snipe! Nick, I can't put it into words really, it was one of them 'you had to be there' moments.

Many thanks,
Richard

15/12/2014

Hi Nick,

Well, what a good weekend. Yesterday we were joined by a wild juvenile tiercel. We have had the pleasure of his company a few times now. This is the tiercel that *Polack* flew the snipe with and killed. Nick Ellison was there that day, with Old Chris and Young. One of the best days hawking I've ever had. This tiercel is not as well-trained as the ones on the other moor, but it's learning the job now. *Todd* was on point, *Polack* was in the right spot. Get in! *Polack* coming down like a train, he clipped the snipe but not fatally, out of nowhere came the wild one and knocked it to the ground. *Polack* took his chance and stole the meal, amazing!! The wild tiercel was not happy, but allowed *Polack* the meal. I left *Polack* to feed up and we went to find a snipe for the wild one. *Todd* locked up and I waited for the tiercel to come round, the peregrines on the other moor know the score and wait on nearly above you, but this youngster was a bit shy. Anyway, Get in! Nick, what a flight, this snipe was in big trouble, it tried to go up, down, anywhere to avoid this relentless tiercel. You will never get a flight like that with a trained hawk, the fitness is unreal. This snipe beat this tiercel to a plantation about a mile away, all watched through the binoculars, truly amazing, it's the only word I can use to do the flight justice.

Five minutes later he was back over us for another do. We walked for a good twenty minutes. Bang, *Todd* was on. This time the tiercel came right above. I honestly thought it was *Polack* above, but *Polack* was now on my fist. Get in *Todd*!! He came down like something possessed, but these snipe are no mugs, I watched the feet come out on the tiercel and he just missed on the strike. This snipe did not want anything to do with this tiercel and bailed instantly. I carried on walking off the moor, but still looking for the wild one, he must have gone I thought. *Todd* locked up, but just seemed a bit different though, so I walked in slowly to see. It was a woodcock. I flushed it and watched it fly off across the moor. I'm sure you know what is coming next, yea you got it, the wild tiercel came in like a bullet, he was all over it, but fair play to the woodcock it jinked its way to the same plantation as the snipe did earlier and made its very lucky escape. I walked off the hill thinking about what I had just witnessed.

Many thanks,

Richard

Snipe became scarce on the hill and *Polack* was left waiting on to be served for long periods. He then started to check and being so efficient it was of little surprise that he ended up killing pigeons in the towns.

31/12/2014

Hi Nick,

Well Nick, we got the bugger, he has been on a right killing spree. When we first slipped him on Pendle he weighed 1 lb 4.5 oz when we picked him up he weighed 1 lb 6.5 oz. We eventually picked *Polack* up 20 mile away from home. *Polack* had moved very early this morning. We had no signal until Chris had a very slight bleep, that was the bleep we needed, he had gone right up the valley skipping the occasional town and trying his luck at anything he fancied. We pinned him down to a town called Colne, It wasn't long before everything feathered was in panic mode, he flew right over mine and Chris's head after a flock of, yea you got it, pigeons. I didn't realize

End of the day

just how many pigeons there are in these towns, my town included, it's black with them. *Polack* was just testing these pigeons, he landed on a roof. We had to take our chance and it paid off, *Polack* is that greedy he could not resist the lure. We had him! The first thing I noticed was he looked like he had had a blood bath. I think another day or two and we would have really struggled.

I would just like to thank Young Chris, he has been at my house every morning at 6 am for the last three mornings. Cheers Chris. I'm out on the rass tonight with Anne and my daughters, content knowing that we got him home safely.

Many thanks,

Richard and Chris

1/1/2015

Marcus was over today. We started with both tiercels on the hill, but there was very low cloud and rain. We had a couple of flights, but nothing special – that low cloud really spoils things. It was time to get the big guns out, *KP* and *Hellboy*, Marcus's gull hawks. We drove around a bit to find the right slip, Marcus was happy and *KP* was sent

140

Son of Hellboy

on her way. *KP* made a kill, but out of sight. *Hellboy* (good name that) was unhooded and Marcus slipped at some gulls about quarter of a mile away. What a good flight. *Hellboy* got above his gull, stooped and hit the gull but not fatally, he wanted this gull now and the flight went out of sight. We tracked him down, he had caught his gull. That's the first time I've watched a gull flight.

1/1/2015

I'm so glad that everyone enjoyed the exploits of *Polack*, but I can't take all the credit. Young Chris has been there from the word go, even when *Polack* was just a grass cutter. We both watched him progress into a very exiting high-flying tiercel. A lot of the best flights we had with him didn't end in kills. It was the stoop and the flight that followed that we wanted to see and when the wild ones appeared, well it was just amazing. Both myself and Chris had a reckoning up today and we think we had about fifty different flights with the wild peregrines. Four other people witnessed the flights, Old Chris and Nick Ellison being two of them. Two friends of mine saw some breath-taking flights, but I don't think they realised what they were watching, not being falconers.

I would just like to thank Old Chris for the pictures. By the way, the reason we called him *Polack* was because of Old Chris being part Polish.

And, of course, to my very understanding wife Anne who knows how dedicated I am.

CHAPTER NINE

Sydney Airport Falcons

by Nick Wilkinson

HAVING BEEN ASKED by Marcus to contribute to his excellent book, I thought back to books I had enjoyed at the start of my falconry career. I enjoyed learning how to be a good falconer, but what interested me most were the stories of falconry and hawks at the back of those books. So with that thought in mind, I dusted off the following story that has lain dormant in my desk for decades.

Sydney Airport, Australia, 1977

In the late seventies I was one of three people to participate in an experiment to control gulls at Sydney International Airport by the use of falcons. For various reasons the project was not a total success and the four peregrines used were, over a three month period, to be hacked back in the area they had been taken as eyasses. One of our number had to return to the UK, leaving myself and another to achieve this task. At this time the peregrines, *Letcher, Leila, Tod* and *Gwen*, although nine months old, had never been entered at quarry. They had, however, been flown each day since being hard-penned.

The spot chosen was called Wizard's Peak, fifteen miles east of Geraldton on the west coast, a beautiful hill some seven hundred feet high. From the top a good view could be had of the coast and landmarks thirty miles away were clearly visible. An afternoon sea breeze and warm hot days gave plenty of lift. In fact, on one occasion it got so windy we tied blankets to our hands and feet and attempted an early form of hang gliding.

The falcons were introduced to the hill over several days before being given total freedom. I elected to live on the hill and my partner came out from town every day with fresh supplies. Four falcons and a man on a hill, pure bliss. The falcons loved their new found freedom, playing on and above the hill to heights where a good pair of binoculars could barely keep them visible, four tiny silhouettes in a clear blue sky. Although they gained great height, they rarely ventured far from the hill in the first week.

Quarry was readily available. Feral pigeons from a local farm and old chapel nearby, cuckoos, parrots, doves in surrounding hedges, and ducks on local dams. Obviously, one would have to write a book on the subject to include all the happenings. Memorable occasions were when cooking breakfast and having four falcons sitting on a log next to me. *Gwen* tail-chasing a pigeon across the hill that suddenly exploded, clouds of feathers in its wake. *Gwen* caught it before it hit the ground and flew around the side of the hill. Rushing to the spot I found five falcons squabbling over the pigeon, one being a haggard falcon that had given the coup-de-grace. The phantom, a haggard tiercel, often stooping past us at such speed wc never did get a good look at him. Four falcons waiting on while I tried to persuade a duck to leave the safety of a dam. A lark hopping through a gate from one side to the other as falcons tried to jump down to catch it. *Tod* and *Letcher* catching a cuckoo between them and on sorting out the tangle, *Letcher* thinking he had the prize flew off dragging *Tod* behind him, when it was me who had the quarry.

Eventually the falcons acquired their skills and would leave the hill, sometimes returning a week or two later looking in good condition. Only *Letcher* never left the hill. Although he was quite capable of looking after himself he had a great attachment to me.

After three months the money ran out and they were left on their own. I suppose it wasn't a fairytale ending for any of them, but better than being put in a zoo, as had been suggested by some people. Having spent three months on the peak with four falcons I saw sights I will never see again and certainly will never forget.

Letcher

Letcher was a tiercel peregrine taken by myself, along with his sister *Leila*, from cliffs at Ellendale Pool east of Geraldton, West Australia, and used in bird control at Sydney airport for nine months of 1977. I was lucky to survive our initial encounter. I arranged to meet the wildlife officer, Les Brown, above the cliff and he said he would acquire some rope from the fisheries department. That rope was rotten, but being the can-do variety of people we quadrupled it, tied it around my waist, and over the cliff I went. Standing on a sandstone ledge being attacked by angry peregrines, whilst placing two eyasses in a sack, while secured by rotten rope was most exciting!

Letcher was my first peregrine, I was in love. Along with three others he was sent to Sydney Airport, where he grew into a fine tiercel. I arrived soon after and took him up and trained him. He was a very dark tiercel, and I doubt you could have found a better one. His first flight was memorable. I released him and up he went, up, up and eventually out of sight. Ten minutes of swinging the lure brought no response. I returned to the mews to get some binoculars, but still no sight was to be had. Twenty minutes after letting him go he returned, a very tired bird. As so often happens on the first flight of a bird reared in an enclosed aviary, he had no idea of how to descend in flight. Only when exhausted did he learn the eventual flying skills that enabled him to return to his place of departure, much to my (and I assume, his) relief.

He was a pleasure to fly and handle, being very tame and perfectly mannered. He was not entered, as his main role in life was to fly about as a deterrent to gulls wanting to cross the runway. Like most young falcons he loved flying and was a constant joy to watch.

The trial contract came to an end when he was about nine months old and he was hacked back to the wild as previously described. For a few months after that I took a job as night stockman at a local abattoir, this enabled me to visit the hill daily. Faithful *Letcher* was always there. Wanting to progress in life, I then bought a digger and went contracting, laying pipeline, for the public works department.

The contract was some hundreds of miles from Geraldton, which meant I was no longer able to visit the hill.

I asked my good friend Rocco to go out daily to feed *Letcher*, although I knew he was well able to feed himself. The first day he went *Letcher* was there, but he was not encountered after that. We later heard a rumour that he had gone into Geraldton and killed a woman's pet parrot in her back garden and she in turn had killed him with a rake. Did he go looking for me, he knew that was where my car came from daily? Who knows? Probably a very sad end to a magnificent falcon.

Leila

A peregrine falcon, taken by myself along with her brother, *Letcher*, from Ellendale Pool east of Geraldton, Western Australia.

Leila was a very dark powerful falcon. Originally she was trained by Bob Hicks, but he had to return to the UK and she came into the possession of Phil Bland, Bob's replacement. Phil was a great character, far older than the rest of us at Sydney. He was an adventurer, had been in the navy, then prospected throughout the south seas with some mates, only to have their boat sunk from under them. He was a true gentleman and *Leila* being his first peregrine, he was as much in love with her as I was with *Letcher*.

Leila was very boisterous and a little noisy, if I remember correctly. While at Sydney she wasn't entered, but undoubtedly knew how to kill. This came about because she went AWOL for a whole week. Phil and I had the evening shift at the time. This meant we went north of the airfield to some sandbanks that the gulls were using to roost. Our job was to prevent roosting. This wasn't some isolated shore; blocks of flats were only yards from where we flew the falcons.

One evening *Leila* disappeared behind these flats and didn't return. Phil was gutted, but came out every night for a week to the flying area, but to no avail. After a week I couldn't persuade him to accompany me any more. He said he would wait in the van while I went up to scare off the gulls. There I was flying *Letcher*, when low and behold in comes *Leila*, now I had my hands full. I managed to get *Letcher* down, hood him, and take up *Leila*. I walked back to the van triumphant, *Letcher* on my arm and *Leila* feeding on my fist. To this day I can envisage the delight on Phil's face, his baby was back.

I don't recall any other significant deeds from *Leila* during those times. The contract finished and she was due to return to West Australia. I travelled over by land, and Phil and Larry were to box up the falcons that were to travel by air to Perth, where I was to collect them. Phil was adamant that nothing would part him from *Leila* and planned to smuggle her back to the UK. Common sense prevailed, twenty four hours on a plane with a noisy falcon stuffed up his jumper wasn't an option, and *Leila* arrived at Perth with the other falcons.

She was soon at hack, but being a bully it was always *Leila* generally causing havoc. Within a couple of months she was spending many days away from the hill, obviously well able to take care of herself. She would return at the most inappropriate times, usually when one of the other falcons was on a kill, beat them up and steal their prize. Finally we decided we had had enough and took her to the Mullewa district some eighty miles away and released her in an agricultural area full of game. We never heard from her again and can only hope she survived.

Tod

A tiercel peregrine taken by myself from Sugarloaf Hill near Northallerton, north of Geraldton, West Australia, and used in bird control at Sydney Airport for nine months of 1977.

Towards the end of the period of hack the falcons, including *Tod*, were often away from the hill for many days. For a few months after that I took a job as night stockman at a local abattoir, this enabled me to visit the hill daily, only occasionally did I encounter *Tod*. The last time I saw him during this period, after his absence of some weeks, I threw out a dead pigeon to which he came down. He looked magnificent, was nearly fully moulted into adult plumage, took a full crop off the fist as calm as you like. I thought that would be the last I saw *Tod*, how wrong I was.

Larry, the other person involved with hacking the falcons, had gone back to Sydney, but after a period of about six months he decided to return to Geraldton. On his second day back he was down town, sitting in a café writing a letter, when he glanced out the window and caught sight of a tiercel chasing a flock of pigeons down the main street. He went out and there was *Tod* sat on a roof top looking down at him. He swears that falcon followed him about town for the rest of the day. He went to a car yard to purchase a car and *Tod* pitched up on the roof. Did he recognise Larry amongst all those people? Who knows?

Word came to us that the local pigeon-racing fraternity was gunning for *Tod* for obvious reasons. He was roosting down at the wharf on the grain silos, and apparently they had him caught under a coat one night, but he managed to escape. Another time some dockers popped a cardboard box over him as he was taking his pleasure on a pigeon. Luckily they told Jim a tug-boat skipper they had this peregrine; Jim being a falconry friend of ours released him. Things were obviously too hot for *Tod* and bound to end in disaster, so Larry hearing about the last box episode took a frozen pigeon from the freezer and went down the wharf. Down came *Tod* as though he had just been lost during flying a few hours previous.

I was due some time off at the end of a contract, so decided to keep him to hand and fly him, but all too soon work beckoned and a decision had to be made. I had a sister who farmed some three hundred miles south east of Perth, so I took *Tod* down there and released him. The last I saw of him was as he flew off into the distance with a Port Lincoln parrot in his feet, being chased by an angry mob of its compatriots.

Gwen

A peregrine falcon taken by myself from Sugarloaf hill near Northallerton, north of Geraldton, West Australia, along with her brother *Tod*.

Gwen was flown by Larry Townsend. I don't recall much about her being flown at Sydney, because I was mostly doing opposite shifts to Larry, so only occasionally saw her airborne. She arrived back in West Australia with the other three and went to the peak for hacking.

During the hack period she suffered a seizure-stroke and became partly paralysed down one side of her body, which resulted in her flying slightly lopsided. Up until this period she was holding her own with the other falcons, but this setback severely restricted her progress. By the end of the hack period it was decided that she should be brought in and retained. Our good friend, Rocco, was prepared to take her on and flew her on a daily basis, until she was eventually lost. This was before the introduction of telemetry.

A concerted effort was made to find her to no avail – we even hired an aircraft. A quick phone call was made to Geraldton Airport and an exorbitant price was quoted to hire a four-seater. I phoned around all my friends and managed to rustle up five others to partake in a little adventure. The plan was for three people to go for the first half hour, then return and swop over for the next three, this reduced the price dramatically. We searched all the local hills, great fun directing the pilot and a very uplifting experience in some of the updrafts. It was enjoyable to see the area from the prospective of a falcon, but again to no avail and *Gwen* was never heard of again.

Emma Peel

Emma was a passage falcon trapped by myself at Sydney. Larry fancied Emma Peel from the Avengers TV series, that's how she got the name. At the end of the contract she was released north of Sydney.

One afternoon Larry came in from the airfield and stated he wanted a creance, as he had spotted a falcon feeding on a wader and planned to wind her up. I had seen a film about sakers in Hungary, where a falcon was caught by someone dug into the ground holding a pigeon, so I suggested we tried this. We only had one pigeon, a very poor bird that could hardly lift its wings, never the less we grabbed it along with a shovel and off we went. We dug a hole close to the runway at the far end of the airfield and in I got, with a bag over my head and two slit holes to see from. Larry covered me in sand, placed the pigeon in my hands, and off he went.

Larry drove towards where he had seen the falcon earlier and found her sitting on the sea wall, having completed her meal. She took off and eventually came into my field of view, climbing away. I gave the pigeon a shake, but got no response as it was such a poor specimen. By holding its feet and pushing its tail back and forward I got it to flap its wings in a very peculiar way. This seemed to have the desired effect and got the attention of the departing falcon. She went out of view, but soon I heard her land close by – she didn't strike the pigeon, just landed nearby. She walked forward and stood on my head, then walked around the pigeon and stood on my feet. She must have wondered what was going on, the ground was heaving up and down with my excited breathing and I was also trying hard to keep my hands out of her sight under the pigeon. After what seem a long time she walked forward, grabbed the pigeon by the neck with her beak and tried to pull it towards my feet. She was still out of reach of my hands. I refused to let go the pigeon and she eventually footed it. Quick as a flash I grabbed her foot, had her securely and sat up, I must have scared her half to death. Larry collected me and off we went back victorious to hood and jess our prize. Larry trained and flew her, but it wasn't long before the contract finished and she was released.

Black Falcons

We had some black falcons that Tony Croswell and Larry had trapped in Queensland. I flew a tiercel and Larry and Phil flew falcons. It's a long time ago and I can't quite recall how many there were, probably four in total, nor can I remember any names. Basically they were like black sakers – not a patch on the peregrines. I remember mine catching a few small birds, but we weren't interested in hunting with them, just flying them to deter the gulls. At the end of the contract Larry took a long trip north and released them.

Little Falcons

Also known as the Australian hobby. They are in no way a hobby, far too well-equipped in the feet department for that. I took three from a nest in West Australia around the same time I took the peregrines. Two were tiercels, the other a falcon. They were named *Scotty*, *Howard* and *Arch* after three people at Sydney who were involved with the falcon project. Obviously their size meant they were not much use as gull deterrents. One died from lack of vitamin B, or so the PM said. A further one was lost, just leaving the falcon, *Scotty*. She was returned to West Australia, given to our good friend Paul, and eventually lost while flying at quail near the coast.

Goshawks

We had various goshawks, from white to brown. We trapped some brown ones on the airfield. None were trained to the point of going free, and all were released at the end of the contract.

Young merlins

CHAPTER TEN

Merlin Breeding

by Nick Wilkinson

MARCUS ALSO ASKED me to include a chapter on breeding merlins. I don't claim to be an expert in the breeding of these small falcons, but probably have more experience than anyone in the UK at present. Since we are now completely dependent on captive breeding to provide merlins for falconry in the UK, the future of lark hawking requires that quality merlins are bred in a consistent and sustainable way if the sport is to have a future. Unfortunately, merlins are notoriously tricky to breed successfully – particularly on a long term basis. People ask me how I achieve the task. I tell them it is attention to detail 365 day a year and 366 on a leap year. Occasionally I come across people who tell me the task is easy, but these are usually first time breeders with a lucky pair. A couple of years down the line these people are no longer to be heard of, with the merlin either killing the jack, or all youngsters produced dying from coccidiosis. The long term merlin breeder is a rare individual indeed and one who commands my respect. I will not go into detail about incubation, there is a wealth of knowledge out there regarding this task that explains it far better than I ever could and the prospective merlin breeder should hunt it out, read it, absorb it, understand it and be proficient at it long before they acquires their first valuable fertile merlin eggs. The following are only my own personal views, not instructions for others to necessarily follow. Take from them what you will and good luck if you attempt the task.

Selecting Breeding Stock

Most merlins will breed, I have even heard of imprints breeding as part of a pair. I prefer crèche-reared merlins, but parent-reared breed just as easily. I am unconvinced that a merlin that is imprinted from an egg and never saw another merlin until it was full grown will breed. Most imprinted merlins I know of that have bred were usually left with siblings or parents until ten or twelve days old and I think this is the important difference. I have seen pure imprint merlins that were in aviaries with other merlins that would never breed.

Good jacks can be expected to breed until fourteen years. Good merlins can be expected to breed up until year ten. Poor-producing merlins, or unreliable jacks, need removing from the breeding process.

Breeding Aviaries

Skylight and seclusion aviaries. I have astro-turf/carpet on all perches. I also have small pieces of soft sandstone attached to some perches, to help keep beak and talons down. I have even used an aviary with nothing but sandstone perches, but even this was insufficient to keep beaks and talons in shape. I cope all my merlins about once every three months.

Think where perches are positioned in the aviary. 1,2,3. The jack must be able to take off (1). Then copulate (2). Then fly onto another perch (3).

My nest boxes are approximately 2 feet by 2 feet. They are constructed with a sliding front door that can be lowered by a line from outside the aviary. They also have an outside hinged door, for access from outside the aviary. The internal structure is a trench that goes across the nest-box. It is 6 inches wide, 3 inches deep and at least 6 inches away from the back wall. There is carpet on the base of the trench. The trench is filled with gravel or grit. The grit should not be too small in diameter, or it will not hold the eggs in position when the merlin turns them and you will end up with egg migration. Eggs will then be left out by incubating merlins to chill and this will result in addled eggs. Besides the trench, the remainder of the internal area is wood level with the top of the trench.

I believe the advantages of nest boxes are the following. The eggs will be protected from outside influences. If anything upsets the merlins like crows, sparrowhawks, buzzards, cats, you name it, the merlins will not be crashing about the aviary and landing on eggs, cracking eggs. The merlin incubating will feel very secure and not be able to see hazards as described that might make it bolt the eggs. If the incubating merlin does leave the box to investigate the alarm call by its mate, the eggs will remain protected within the box. Merlins can be locked out by lowering the door when they leave the nest box and this will allow eggs to be checked, taken, without undue stress to both the merlin and the breeder. Boxes are constructed from plywood and placed out of direct sunlight. It is important that they are in a dry area, well ventilated and waterproof.

Consider placing a small-mesh 8-inch high window in aviary that looks out onto garden. This will allow nervous birds to become familiar with their environment and at ease with noises etc. Close the window about a month before eggs are expected, so they concentrate on breeding and don't become distracted by activity outside the aviary.

Perches should be 2½ inches wide. Any less than this, the merlins will have difficulty balancing while eating food and will take their food to the aviary floor to eat.

I keep all pairs separated outside the breeding season. This is achieved by making the aviary in two halves with a wired door between them.

So to the aviary. A square, 3 metres, by 3 metres, by 2 metres high. Two ends would be covered in tin just under 1 metre wide (overlap to prevent rain getting in will use some of the 1 metre wide tin), so only a one metre and a bit gap in the middle open to the elements. There would be a dividing wall down the middle, from covered end to covered end, with a dividing door in the middle of the wall. This door would be slightly less than 1 metre wide, a wire door. It would be a sliding door. If you make it swinging it takes up a lot of aviary space to open it. One corner of the aviary would have a double entrance door.

This door would only take up a small corner of one of the halves, just enough to get in and close the outside door, before opening the internal door. All perches, baths, nest boxes, ledges would be exactly the same height about 4 feet, leaving about 2 ft 6 ins from perch to top of roof, high enough for merlins to fly without restricting them, especially when copulating. Food platforms would be at the end of a perch. By keeping everything at the same height, there is little reason for merlins to descend to the aviary floor, keeping them away from the dreaded coccidia. The feed shoot will be a 90 degree plastic bend, the type used for gutter piping. There will be a merlin ladder in each aviary for feather clipped or damaged merlins to climb back up, if they end up on the floor. No perch will be further than 1 metre from the next perch, the distance a merlin can easily jump. Perches should be high enough to get merlins up into the sunshine. There will be a bath in each aviary filled and emptied from outside the aviary via a hose that comes from the base of the bath through the tin. The aviary would need to be positioned in a certain position to prevent sunlight shining on the nest box. On a still hot day you will be amazed how the sun can heat things up.

The aviary must have double netting on the top, to prevent sparrowhawk attacks. When a sparrowhawk attacks during the breeding season, the jack will go up to fend it off and may become damaged in his attempts.

Food And Medication

I worm adults using 'Harker's HARKA-MECTIN Spot On Endectocide' for pigeons, about twice a year. First application during early January and again after the breeding season is complete, around beginning of August.

Coccidia: Why do merlins suffer from coccidia far more than any other falcon? Could the answer be that they feed on the floor of an aviary rather than eat their food from perches. Could the solution be to ensure the food placed in a merlin's aviary is in portions small enough so they can eat it from a perch? I have noticed if I give a day-old turkey chick to merlins they take it to the floor to eat. If I cut it into three, they eat it from perches. I feed all food to merlins in sizes that can be eaten from perches.

Day-old chicken chicks: I remove feet, part of egg yolk and cut into two.

Day-old turkey chicks: I remove feet, part of egg yolk and cut into three.

Prime quail: I remove intestines, feet, beak, cut in half from front to back and smash bones. Head and neck one piece, two remaining sides cut into seven pieces each, so fifteen pieces in total.

Pigeons: I skin to remove all fat, remove intestines, feet, wings, head, backbone, parson's nose. Split in half, removing breast bone keel and any fat. Smash with axe and depending on size of pigeon cut each half on average into ten pieces, total twenty. Warning, such small pieces can dry out quickly during hot weather. I mash some feathers into the meat for casting.

Coccidiosis Management In Breeding Merlins

These are my own personal notes for the management of coccidia in my own merlins from observations I have made. These are not recommendations on how people should control coccidia in merlins.

Coccidia is species-specific, the type of coccidia in merlins being different from, say, turkey or chicken. It is known that chickens have seven different types of coccidia, but only two types are particularly troublesome.

From my understanding and observations coccidia is the equivalent to the sore throat virus in humans. It is permanently present, but only troublesome and flares up during times of stress. Breeding merlins coming up to egg-laying and during egg-laying must be considered to be in times of stress. I often hear cases of merlins laying two or three eggs and dying. In my opinion the majority of deaths in these birds is probably coccidia.

What I am fairly sure of is that Coxitabs, used to control coccidia in pigeons, also works for merlins and is very safe to use. I have seen remarkable effects from administering Coxitabs to sick merlins that I assume were suffering from coccidia. I also have witness accounts from other people who have treated severe cases of coccidia in merlins to good effect.

So let's assume that Coxitab is very effective in controlling coccidia in merlins. Let's also assume that most merlins kept in aviaries for many years are infected with coccidia. Merlins build up immunity to coccidia, but this immunity is at times of stress insufficient and an attack can occur.

If merlins have immunity to coccidia, why is there a need to medicate? Trials I am doing suggest that if the gut of the merlin can be cleared of coccidian, this might protect the merlin during the period of stress, egg-laying. If the resident coccidia are removed and strict hygiene control is followed there will be insufficient coccidia present to multiply to levels that the merlin immune-system is overrun and an attack will occur. My understanding is that clearing the gut will not affect the immunity the merlin has to coccidia.

So to medication:

Studying the life cycle of coccidia and from observations and trials, the best I can come up with is: one half a tablet every fourth day throughout the egg-laying period. I start Coxitabs on 1st April and finish when the last egg is laid. Other people have trialled a full tablet every third day to equally good results. At present I am just medicating the merlin, not the jack. After all, I have never heard of a merlin laying three eggs and the jack dying.

How to administer:

Simply crush up a Coxitab tablet and sprinkle it on food. The tablet has no taste whatsoever and when sprinkled on day-old chick the merlin is not aware of its presence. I think it's most beneficial to administer on one piece of food, at the first feed of the day, if you are confident the merlin will get the medicated portion. Mostly the jack will deliver the first piece of food to the merlin. However, I have often had a jack eat two tablets and the merlin none when trying this procedure.

Coccidia cannot be *eradicated* by chemicals – all you can hope for is a degree of control. No amount of bleach, Jeyes Fluid or other products will eradicate it. Pigeon people try to get rid of it by using blow torches, probably why so many lofts burn down. They routinely medicate.

All the above are just my thoughts on the subject, I might have it wrong. However, the evidence over the last few years leads me to think I'm on the right track. It will take a few more years to come to the correct conclusions. This is my thinking at present, not recommendations. I have never known Coxitabs to have a detrimental effect on any merlin, or eggs produced by medicated merlins.

Feeding

Feed breeding adults highest quality food during and before the breeding season. We have all heard of someone who has a pair of kestrels, that were fed nothing but chicks and they laid, hatched, five eggs and reared them all. It might work for kestrels, it doesn't work for merlins. I and other people have tried it with disastrous results. I have also trialled nothing but pigeon with equally disastrous results.

Success depends on top quality food. From beginning of March, until the end of egg-laying I feed a four-day cycle, 1 day small quail, 1 day chicks plus Raptors Essentials, 1 day skinned pigeon, 1 day chicks, plus half a Coxitab for merlin, back to start. During the rest of the year I am more flexible with the diet. I used to feed each type of food in three day blocks during the breeding season, but this produced an uneven set of chicks, some very weak.

I have seen food being dragged across eggs. I have often seen this when jacks take food to merlins for nest change-over, it gets dragged across, placed upon the eggs. Could it be the reason for so many eggs failing during incubation, from clutches taken? A piece of quail that has liver hanging from it does make quite a splash on an egg it has been dragged across. Do not feed any food that can contaminate eggs during the incubation period, pigeon/quail with wet liver attached for instance, or chicks with egg yolk hanging out the back end. Egg yolk especially can block pores on the egg. This will prevent the embryo developing within the egg and result in the death of the chick within the egg.

Preparing For Breeding Season

I let merlins together about the middle of March. I feather-clip all merlins, even merlins from first-year pairs. I clip off all primaries from one wing of the merlin, in line with secondaries, and every other tail feather before letting her in with the jack. This will allow her to get about, even when she starts to moult, but hopefully prevent her catching and killing the jack. No matter how docile she has been in previous year, she may turn on the jack. You do not want to be clipping feathers when the merlin is about to lay eggs. Ramps will need to be placed in aviaries and perches need to be no further apart than one metre. A merlin heavy with eggs and wet after a bath with wings clipped will have difficulty getting about and must be able to walk to every part of the aviary. Be sure to cut back beaks and talons when letting the pair together. The merlin's talons especially should be cut back as far as is safe, jacks are killed by these daggers. This should be a quick operation performed with a small pair of nail clippers. If you prolong this by using files etc, you risk the bird dying from heart attack. Merlins wrapped in towels can soon overheat. I hold my merlins in bare hands.

Dangerous Time

From introduction until the first egg is laid is probably the most dangerous time for the jack. I don't think these merlins that kill jacks mean to. I think they are probably annoyed with the jack for various reasons and just want to give him a good kicking, but most have overgrown talons and these daggers do the damage. I do think that some merlins don't recognize jacks that have had a good bath and especially during the breeding season, she will want him (to her an intruder) out of her territory. In this scenario she might want to kill him, but again I think she probably just want him gone, which is impossible in an aviary situation. As long as the merlin is feather-clipped in the correct manner, she should not be able to catch even a wet jack. I usually find once the first egg is laid things settle down.

Young pairs in their first year may become restless in an aviary for a few weeks before eggs appear. From observations I think the cause is that they feel the urge to breed and wish to find a suitable territory. After a period of time they realize there is no escape from the aviary and are forced to accept the aviary as a breeding territory. I have only witnessed this behaviour in first-year breeders and it is usually a good sign that breeding may occur that year.

Eggs

Even with first-year breeders I double-clutch. I take eggs ten days after last egg laid for clutches up to four eggs. If I have a five eggs first clutch I take eggs fifteen days after last egg laid, allowing the merlin a longer period to recover before laying a second clutch. Double-clutching is acceptable, triple clutching isn't. Triple clutching puts added stress on the merlin, and could cause its death. You might want to leave second clutches with parents until the pip stage. They don't have power failures and any resulting chicks may be stronger and more vigorous than those hatched in incubators.

Addled eggs might also be caused by the jacks incubating eggs as they are laid, when the merlin is just covering eggs before she starts to incubate once the clutch is nearly complete. Jacks don't cover/stand over eggs, they are only programmed to incubate. In the early stages of the clutch building the wild jacks are rarely seen at the nest except for brief food drops, or anti-corvid air cover triggered by the merlin alarm-calling. It is logical therefore that jacks may start eggs that are then lost because they are not incubated by the merlin. To combat this, in pairs that produce addled eggs, it might be advisable to take each egg as laid, replacing it with a dummy egg. These eggs can then be stored and returned once the clutch has been completed for natural incubation. If this course of action is followed you would need easy access to the eggs, by way of a nest box with an external door/hatch.

Aggression In Breeding Merlins

Out of all the conundrums that need to be worked through, regarding merlin breeding, aggression has to be the most difficult to understand and combat. The trouble is, there isn't just one cause of aggression, there are many. Not only are there many, there are different degrees of aggression, from very mild, which is nothing to worry about, to severe, that might end in the death of the jack, or merlin. What the merlin breeder needs to understand is the predicament we place merlins in, when we restrict them to a confined aviary in which to breed. To understand the problem we must first know the process in which the wild merlins breed.

The jack arrives on the breeding territory, sometime in March. He sets up a territory into which he hopes to attract a mate. He defends that territory. The merlin arrives, thinks he is a handsome fellah and decides he is for her. Courtship follows, he feeds her, etc, etc. She can see he is a good provider and decides to breed. The size of the clutch will probably depend on the amount of food the jack can provide. Eggs form within the merlin's body and she is incapable of hunting. The jack is kept busy, fully occupied, providing for his new wife. The merlin decides that it is time to have her eggs fertilized and allows copulation. The jack is so busy providing food, chasing off crows, etc, he has to find time to copulate.

The first egg is laid. Now he is really busy, providing enough food for himself and the merlin, who eats far more when egg production is underway, and not forgetting to copulate, when he has time between chasing off predators. Over a few days the clutch is completed, the merlin settles down to incubation. The jack occasionally takes over incubation duties to allow her to feed, mute, preen, etc. He can't spend too long at the nest – he is very busy.

The eggs pip, start to hatch. The jack hears the arrival of his offspring. His instincts kick in, all he hears in his head is catch and stash food, catch and stash food. He needs food stored in case of bad weather, besides the food he delivers fresh. Mostly, the merlin feeds the young until they are a bit older. That is her job, his is to provide the food.

All goes well, the jack chases off predators, crows, buzzards, harriers, etc. The family fledge, the merlins teach their offspring the ways of survival and they all eventually depart the area for another year. You can see the jack has been a very busy individual indeed.

Now take that jack and place him in an aviary with a merlin, probably not a jack of her choice. The merlin says to the jack, "Right, where is my lovely nest you are supposed to provide?" If it is a reasonable nest she begrudgingly agrees. If not she says to the jack, "Is that the best you can do! I'm not putting up with that! Go find somewhere better and stop spending all day staring at me!!" Poor old jack can't. Well, she isn't putting up with that and starts chasing him, to get him to go off and fulfil her aspirations of a nice stately home, fit for purpose. This aggression can be severe. She finally accepts that the nest he has chosen is the best she is going to get, or she might make her own nest. It is the merlin that chooses the nesting area, no matter what the jack might think.

Food is plentiful and he doesn't even have to go catch it. He collects food and carries it about the aviary pretending he caught it. I don't expect the merlin is that impressed, but she decides she will lay some eggs. Eggs develop. Our jack is bored to tears, he starts thinking about sex. Well, there isn't much else to do, except watch the sky and that is pretty boring. When a crow lands in a tree, near by, the merlin gives her alarm call and expects him to go chase it off. "What use are you, you won't even chase that crow away and if you want sex, you can think again! You can only have sex when I am ready and not before!" The trouble is that is all he thinks about, well it is boring being a jack without a job. This state of affairs can cause sexual aggression, usually not too severe. However, I had one proven jack in with a first year merlin. The merlin wouldn't stand for copulation. The jack was so relentless in his attempts to copulate he ended up killing the merlin. He attacked her so often, that when the egg was far down in the oviduct it broke and caused the death of the merlin. He then copulated upon the dead body. Jacks obviously have no shame.

Eggs develop within the merlin and eventually she allows copulation. Eggs finally appear and things settle down. In the wild the jack would be busy, as previously described, but he is bored, bored, bored. He sees the egg and decides to incubate. Not his job, but it relieves the boredom. The trouble is that jacks aren't programmed to cover eggs, they only incubate. They shouldn't be near the nest at the egg-laying stage. This activity can result in the jack killing the eggs by incubating them, then letting them cool. Eggs can withstand a certain amount of this activity, but a persistent jack can spoil the eggs.

Eventually the eggs pip, hatch. Our jack now hears the young calling, his instincts kicks in. Catch and stash food! Catch and stash food! He can't get out of the aviary!! Eventually his instincts take over and the only place he can find prey is in the nest, so he necks the chicks and stashes them about the aviary, obviously feeling very proud of himself. The breeder curses the jack and decides to give up trying to breed merlins.

I trialed a new nest box design during 2016. This was the key that opened, in my opinion, the door to me understanding merlin aggression. Sometimes it is the experiments that go wrong that are the best. I was having the worst aggression in my breeding pairs I had ever experienced. I monitor the breeding behaviour of another thirteen pairs, besides my own. No one else was reporting aggression that year, to the extent it appeared in my pairs. The only difference was my new nest area, within the nest box, constructed to restrict the merlins to an 8 X 8 inch square in the corner of the nest box. It became obvious this was not acceptable to the merlins and was the cause of severe aggression at the start of the breeding season. I expanded the area available to the merlins to make a nest and aggression diminished. I did have one year, 2011, when I had no aggression with my merlins. Because I keep detailed notes, I was able to summarize that the reason was because I had provided nest areas that the merlins were pleased with. Once I understood that, it became possible to understand the aggression I had seen and in other circumstances.

One form of aggression that can be extreme is aggression towards the jack from the merlin when the jack has had a bath. People speculate that this aggression is because the merlin sees the jack as vulnerable and she is able to catch and kill him. In my opinion such conjecture is wrong. I am of the opinion that when the jack has a bath, the merlin does not recognize him. To her he is an intruder, close to her nest. She thinks, "Where is my bloody husband when you need him! Why doesn't he get rid of this intruder! I will have to do it myself!" She can't chase him off, this intruder, so she might kill him. In the wild, would a merlin see her mate have a bath? No. If the jack bathed, he would be on the moor somewhere, not in front of his incubating merlin. The only protection, in these circumstances, is the fact that the merlin is feather-clipped and unable to catch even a wet jack. A simple solution to the problem is to build the nest box with the entrance facing towards a corner, or a wall, so that the incubating merlin cannot see the wet jack. It is not always the merlin chasing the jack. A jack will sometimes chase a wet merlin, for the same reason. Another solution is to fill the bath with large gravel or small stones that only allow the merlins to drink, which is very important during breeding. Merlins must not be left without water, especially during egg-laying.

People give falcons feelings. They think merlins will like their offspring. They are wrong, merlins, nor any other falcon has feelings, they only have instinct. There is no need to leave merlin chicks for the adults to rear, but more often than not, eat. They do not need to rear chicks to be a successful breeding pair. I have had merlins double-clutch every year for ten years that never saw a chick. I once saw a merlin, in about year six, trying to feed some food to the second egg she had laid in the second clutch. The reason? She could hear merlin chicks that had been placed in an adjoining aviary. Pure instinct. She heard chicks and instinct told her to feed them, an egg was all that was available. She had never seen a chick in her life. I could relate many more examples of instinct in falcons.

The answers to aggression are manifold. Start by constructing correctly proportioned aviaries. Nest boxes should be fitted out with the correct internal design. Feed the correct food in the correct quantities. Aggression will always be part of breeding merlins. The merlin breeder needs to prepare for it and the only way I know how is to feather-clip the merlin in such a way that she cannot catch the jack, as described in the previous article. The talons also need clipping back as far as is safe.

Incubation

Merlin eggs typically require 28.5 (can be 27 to 31) days to pip. Start timing incubation of a clutch 48 hours before last egg laid, so an egg taken at 10 days since last egg laid is estimated to have had 12 days incubation. Do not think merlins are incubating just because they are covering eggs. However, keep a close watch coming up to hatch. I have known merlins to start incubating from egg one, especially during second clutches.

I used to have malpositioned chicks within eggs at hatch. For instance chicks with their head up wrong end of shell, or their head stuck under their wing, preventing them from pipping and resulting in the death of the chick. Some merlin eggs tend to be elongated, making the centre of gravity different from say a normal large falcon egg. I think I have cured this problem by incubating eggs at a better angle within the incubator. My eggs used to sit on a flat surface. I have now altered the surface so that the eggs now incubate more point end down, blunt end uppermost, as one suspects they would sit under the wild merlin in a moorland nest. To date this experiment has achieved all eggs pipping at the correct position.

Rearing Chicks

I never have, nor will I ever put a merlin chick back with parents. To prevent chicks falling on their backs or splaying their legs during first few days, sellotape towel onto outside of container, so that it is suspended inside the container in a bowl shape. Cut out circles of rough towel to place in the container. The towel can then be changed as it becomes soiled. At about day six, or longer, change to container with wood shavings in heat box. Do this at the start of day, as chicks will often fall onto their backs during the first 24 to 48 hours, until they get their balance. Do not do it when you cannot monitor the situation.

Only feed chicks to proven feed regime, or you kill them. Keep a detailed record of time chick hatches, first feed, etc., until it is in a routine and feeding well. When feeding lots of chicks together, it is easy to lose track of chicks fed and the result is tragedy.

The first feed: Be careful here, not all chicks are the same. I have read papers that say first feed at twenty four hours after hatch. However, it all depends on the strength of the chick that hatches and whether it is hydrated. A chick that has been incubated in an egg that has lost 18% to pip is not going to be as hydrated and strong as a chick that has been incubated by the parents and only lost 15% to pip. If it is a weak dehydrated chick, it will need feeding earlier.

I do not go beyond twelve hours after hatch to first feed. I have experimented feeding longer periods after hatch, up to nineteen hours, it ended in disaster. Keep the food moist, but no so moist you drown the poor little mite. Before each feed lay chick on its back in your hand. Once it has stopped struggling poke tummy with finger. If it is soft, it is fairly safe to feed chick.

From the start of feeding you need to make an assessment at each feed. Is the tummy taut, with grey matter present when you are about to feed, and the chick slow to feed? If the answer is yes, you are probably overfeeding. Is the tummy wrinkled and soft to the touch and the chick screaming for food? If the answer is yes you might be underfeeding. It is a judgment that needs making for each chick at each feed for the first three days. All chicks are not the same.

After the first feed I feed every six hours on the dot, until they are feeding themselves from a bowl. The advantage of feeding every six hours is that it is very difficult to overfeed. It is very easy to underfeed.

When feeding six hourly it has been described as sticking a pencil down the chicks crop, because you need to fill them up so full. I used to feed every five hours and it was very easy to overfeed using that time scale.

First 24 hrs of feeding, day old chicken chick, thigh flesh only.

Day two, my mix is one prime quail with one day-old chicken chick, egg yolk left in. The quail, skin, remove any fat, intestines, the backbone, the neck and head, to reduce amount of bone, leave in liver and heart. Mince, mix through fine hand-mincer or liquidize, obviously remove any large bones when feeding.

Day six onwards, my mix is one prime quail, one feral pigeon (roughly the same size as quail), two day-old chicken chicks with yolk. The pigeon is prepared in exactly the same way as the quail. *No fat at all!!* Obviously no casting in any form.

Day seventeen onwards, my mix is roughly one third chicks, one third wood pigeon, one third prime quail. I use common sense. I leave some egg yolks in, not all. I skin quail, leave a little fat on. I skin pigeons, remove all the fat.

The following is important! Prepare the wood pigeon in this way only, or you will kill the chicks!

Remove all fat and skin. Only use the breast and legs. Slice off the breast and leg meat in tiny slithers to be sure there is no shot of any kind. Remember, someone might have shot it with a shotgun, before you shot it with an air rifle. This is best done when the pigeon is still slightly frozen. Do the same with the heart and liver. Obviously any pigeon in poor condition needs discarding. The only bones I add from the pigeon are the two legs.

I do not add casting until after day fourteen, when they are feeding independently from a bowl. Keep all food moist, but not saturated. Merlins can be very successfully reared by feeding nothing other than prime quail. Mutes should be black and white. If they turn to yellow-brown or come out runny or in sausage form you are feeding the wrong food. Signs to look for are the chicks complaining after being fed and progressively becoming listless and slow to feed. If this is happening, you have the food mix wrong and are slowly killing them.

Hard dry mutes indicates dehydration, add more moisture to mix, or place chicks in a more humid environment.

How do I rear my chicks so they don't scream? From day eight onwards they are kept behind a screen. I use socks on my hands when feeding them, I don't want them imprinting on a hand or a glove. They are trained to beg downwards and will eventually feed readily from a bowl, once they can focus well enough. How do I stay clear of the dreaded cocci? I feed them minced food, all from a bowl until they are practically hard-penned. I don't want them dragging food about their platform, standing in and eating contaminated mutes. Once they are flying around the aviary, they then progress to a piece of plywood on the aviary floor underneath the crèche rearing ledge, that day-old chicks are tied to. This board is introduced by way of a hatch from outside the aviary. Because it is under the platform, no merlin can mute on it from above.

Every merlin that leaves here is given a ten day course of Coxitabs to see it over the initial training period, starting the day it is taken from the aviary. That is four tablets in total.

Tips

- Just because you have a fertile egg it doesn't mean it will hatch, it has to be a quality egg from good quality parents that have been fed on good quality food and even then there are lots of ways to mess things up.
- Use plastic pigeon eggs as replacement for merlin's eggs, the type that split in middle. Fill with fine gravel or sand, glue together, then colour with nail varnish. Merlins can easily sit a second clutch for sixty days.
- When chicks hatch, place them in individual containers for first three days. Write on the container time of hatch. Each time you feed one you can refresh yourself as to when it hatched and write down how it fed, how much it ate, how strong it was. This is important as you are slowly upping the food at each feed, until at day three you feed a small crop.

- Don't rush. Think before you act. It is impossible to retrieve food from a chick's crop once you have fed it. It isn't a race to see how fast you can fill a chick up, take your time when feeding. I have only choked a chick to death once, but I have come close hundreds of times!

- To sex merlins, look at feet at about twelve days or more. Merlins have greenish feet, jacks feet are more a pink colour. Put P-rings on no later than six days.

- I used to catch up merlins between clutches, do beaks/talons, place them in boxes and clean out aviaries. I now think this is a bad idea. I will still do beaks and talons if necessary, but I will not clean out aviaries. The reason? Coccidia - remember it is in the dust and you are just stirring the pot. Far better to clean out after the breeding season, when you part the pair.

- Merlin chicks wings can look like they are deformed, 'Angel Wing', or the like. The primaries will end up on top of the secondaries, it does look weird and deformed. I have had this happen many times. If left alone the wing will always return to the correct position. It might be just a week before the chick is hard-penned, but it will happen. Well, it always has in the past. The cause could be damage to the wing when lifting young chicks from above. Lift them from below, or lift them by the head and let the body swing into the palm of your hand. Another cause might be too high a temperature in the brooder, the first week after hatch.

Twelve ways to kill a merlin

1. Not weighing egg and hoping it loses correct weight to pip.
2. Trying to help an egg hatch that doesn't need it.
3. Delaying helping an egg hatch that does need it.
4. Returning young to adults.
5. Taking chicks off heat too early, placing them in large box so one can crawl away from siblings to get stuck in a corner and chill.
6. Feeding the wrong food to chicks and over-feeding during the first few days.

7. Leaving young merlins unattended in box without wire on top – cats love them.
8. Not bothering to clip feathers off merlin when introduced to jack and allowing talons to grow long and sharp on an aggressive female.
9. Incorrectly numbering food hatches, so when leaving instructions for someone to feed your merlins they don't get fed.
10. Feeding food to chicks that is too wet so they get water in their lungs, die of pneumonia, or drown.
11. Blocking out on lawn in an unprotected area. Foxes, sparrowhawks, tawny owls, cats, all love them – and not in a good way.
12. Never, ever give a merlin rabbit.

Don't forget, it is all about attention to detail 365 days a year, 366 in a leap year. It all sounds reasonable in theory, it is putting it into practice that is the difficult part.

A Typical Merlin Story

I have a friend called Joe. When I got his email one day saying he had a chick dying at eight days old alarm bells went off. I emailed back and said it sounded like his food mix was wrong. He emailed back saying the other five were OK, but he had overfed the eldest two, one had recovered, the other hadn't and died over a three day period. I again voiced my concern, but he said he was following the mix he had used successfully in years past and it was definitely a case of overfeeding. This is what happened.

One weekend he goes to a wedding leaving his son to feed the merlins. His son phones to say he has run out of food, should he mince up some more. No says Joe, just feed quail breast. Joe gets home Sunday night, feeds them while talking to friends, gets distracted, in his opinion overfeeds them. Two eldest go sick, one dies, the other then recovers slowly over a few days, but still isn't right. Now the next four are getting to eight days, they start being slow to feed and complaining. Joe has learned his lesson; he isn't going to overfeed these.

He knows things aren't right, but can't put his finger on it. Emails me and asks if it is OK to add tap water to feed. He says the only difference this year is he has added tap water instead of bottled water he used in the past. I am hearing klaxons going off by now and suggest he phone me ASAP.

So Joe, has the feed mix changed at all? Yes my son fed just breast of quail for a day, now the feed is back to normal, but things are getting worse. Are you sure you are using the same mix that worked in the past? Yes exactly the same mix. Are you sure you haven't made a change in the mix that worked well in previous years, are the quail from a different source? No everything is the same. You are sure you haven't changed anything at all? Well, yes I now only feed four times a day, I used to feed five times a day. BINGO!!

Because of the pressure of work, he had changed to four times a day feeding. Because he was so scared of overfeeding, he underfed. Some people can get away with four times a day, but you need to fill them to the gunnels and then some. Once they came up to eight days, growing fast, they are not getting enough nutrients from Joe, because he is being cautious about overfeeding them.

The only advice I could give was start feeding a mix with plenty of bone, add supplements, feed little and often until back on track. (When Joe minces up a quail he removes the leg bones, because someone told him they splinter and are dangerous. This was bad advice reducing the calcium the chicks were fed.) It is very difficult to recover merlins once a mistake is made. It is best to learn from other peoples mistakes. Joe was unable to save them.

I've been in his position more times than I like to remember. Painful apprenticeship, this merlin breeding – far better to lean from other people's mistakes.

Summary

1. The most important piece of information is that it mostly happens in the aviary. If you don't get that right, you may just as well not bother. Merlins need to be in good health, fed on the correct diet,

to achieve strong, viable fertile eggs that will hatch and rear well.

2. The aviary design has to be correct. Ignore that at your peril.

3. The merlin needs correct feather-clipping to prevent her from killing the jack. This is why aviary design is so important. A heavily clipped merlin, heavy with eggs, wet from a bath, needs to be able to walk to every part of the aviary. If she ends up on the aviary floor, she must be able to climb up to perches and then walk to the nest.

4. Medication is another important aspect. Before and during egg laying the merlin especially needs medicating to prevent a buildup of coccidia. I do not medicate outside the breeding season for coccidia.

5. Leave eggs with merlins for 10 days after last egg laid from a clutch, before taking them to the incubator, 15 days for 5 egg clutches. Only double-clutch, do not triple-clutch.

6. When you take the second clutch of eggs, replace them with dummy eggs. Merlins can easily sit a second clutch of eggs for 60 days. Do not take the dummy eggs away too early.

7. Use quality incubators. You spend a lot of time and effort getting good quality eggs, don't compromise by then using cheap poor-quality incubators. Saying that, the most expensive incubator in the world will not help if the egg is poor quality, but a cheap reliable incubator will hatch a quality egg. Angle eggs within the incubator, point end down, round end uppermost.

8. Become competent in egg weight manipulation. Practice before you get your valuable merlin eggs, do not practice on those.

9. Ensure you have a reliable dedicated hatcher set at the correct temperature and humidity. Read up on hatching the egg and don't start panicking, it is a time to be very patient.

10. Ensure you understand the brooder requirements for newly-hatched chicks. Watch them closely at this time. They will soon tell you if you have it wrong.

11. Read up on how to feed the chicks from the very start. Make your own notes and stick to them. The quality of food fed to chicks dictates the quality of the grown merlin and your reputation as a breeder.

12. Keep your eye on the ball at all times. You cannot write down too many details. When things start to go wrong and you begin to lose the plot you can refer to those note and regain the plot.
13. It is all about attention to detail. Start trying to cut corners and you are heading on the road to ruin.

There is nothing more annoying than people taking home a perfectly healthy young merlin only to phone up a fortnight later to state that it had died, usually just before it was to be flown free. To try to prevent such tragedies I now send every merlin away with the following notes. I may be teaching the experienced merlin-man to suck eggs, but even the best can become complacent. Every young merlin that goes for training starts a ten day course of Coxitabs as soon as it is taken from the aviary, to protect it during the stressful period. Four tablets are administered, the first tablet is administered as soon the merlin is taken from the aviary and then one tablet every third day thereafter.

Top tips from those who know

- These small falcons need one to one attention all the time, especially in flying condition, no other distractions should get in the way of this. They need 100% attention. If one cannot reasonably guarantee this, then one should seriously reconsider taking one on.
- All the standard checks should be performed daily: alertness, bright-eyed, strong healthy rousing, preening, mutes, and castings. Regular condition checks should take place throughout the day. Remember the merlin has a very fast metabolism everything happens in *Fast* time.
- There is literally a very small margin of error with merlins. Falconers who have only flown the larger falcons & accipiters must be aware of this. The husbandry with merlins becomes critical due to the fast metabolism and relatively small weights involved. Merlins will not tolerate being stripped in weight fast and over short

time period, do it slowly and small amounts. It's important to get sufficient food through the gut regularly and consistently, this helps with the appetite, which in turn is required for training and performance. A merlin with a full crop, when left hooded, won't pass over the crop to the gut and into the body where it is needed as quickly as a merlin 'bare faced'. It is essential that the food intake is allowed to pass through the digestive system without restriction. Be aware of ambient temperatures especially during weight reduction and training.

- It is essential to weigh and check the condition of the merlin regularly; you cannot weigh them too often. One needs to be vigilant and ready to correct any problems immediately. Merlins will not give you much time to sort things out. Everything happens, usually in a series of decaying events and *Very, Very Fast,* but takes a long time to correct (if it can be done) and bring the merlin back into good health. If one gets it wrong the flight program is stalled and more importantly the merlin may die.

- It is important to use the same unit of food type (preferably day-old chicks), to accurately control weight and health of the merlin. It's strongly advised to weigh the unit of food given and therefore accurately control weight and condition. Be aware of the different types of food given, as they all have different effects on merlins. You might think quail is best, but quail breast meat on its own is a very white meat, and without the bones, heart and liver of a quail it is not recommended. Try not to make too many erratic changes – consistency is important.

- During the end of training, don't think that you need to reduce weight to encourage them to come to the lure better. A quote from a top merlin man was, 'She came 5 ft to the lure the first night, 5 yds the second night, the full length of the creance the third night, we flew her free on the fourth night and her weight remained exactly the same throughout'.

- Be aware that during the beginning of training the merlin is at 'Basal' state, that is the state the body is in when NOT BURNING ENERGY. The body is at the rested state keeping the internal organs operating normally and alive, i.e. not flying.

The merlin will require more food on top of the 'Basal' state for any increase in energy used, e.g. increased flying distances and exercise. Merlins need added fuel/food to compensate for energy exertion used. This becomes even more critical later when the merlin is flying very hard at fit larks and this may be exacerbated by a drop in ambient temperatures.

- Always err on the side of caution. It is far better to overfeed and fly later, or even miss a day, than to kill your merlin.
- Stay — VIGILANT — VIGILANT — VIGILANT

I hope that this may be useful. I do not want to come across as lecturing. Most experienced falconers are aware of all these things.

"Stay awa' fra' they falconers, Susan,
all they cares abouts is their 'awks."

A woman's advice to her daughter as she stood at the garden gate
making furtive glances at passing members of the O.H.C